# Teaching Students to
# MAKE WRITING VISUAL & VIVID

*Lessons and Strategies for Helping Students Elaborate
Using Imagery, Anecdotes, Dialogue, Figurative Language,
Cinematic Techniques, Scenarios, and Sensory Details*

## David Lee Finkle

**■SCHOLASTIC**

New York • Toronto • London • Auckland • Sydney
Mexico City • New Delhi • Hong Kong • Buenos Aires

## DEDICATION:

For Christopher and Alexandra, the real Tom and Jen, who at the ages of four and five demanded to be in the comic strip. You are more than my kids; you are my students and collaborators, and my pictures of hope.

Editor: Gloria Pipkin
Cover design: Jorge J. Namerow
Interior design: LDL Designs
Copy editor: Jeannie Hutchins

ISBN-13: 978-0-545-14781-1
ISBN-10: 0-545-14781-3
Copyright © 2010 by David Lee Finkle
All rights reserved. Published by Scholastic Inc.
Printed in the U.S.A.
2 3 4 5 6 7 8 9 10    40    17 16 15 14 13 12

# CONTENTS

# ACKNOWLEDGMENTS

Thanks to my wife Andrea for putting up with me and my stressed-out self as my various deadlines loomed. Writing this book was especially challenging because, as I wrote it, I was also drawing cartoons for it that ran in the newspaper first. Thanks to my newspaper editor Nick Klasne, who put up with my running the ragged edge of his deadlines so I could run the ragged edge of the book's deadlines as well. And to Gloria Pipkin for putting up with me running the ragged edge of the book's deadlines so I could meet my newspaper deadlines! Your tireless enthusiasm for my work never fails to make my day.

My students contributed to this book and (mostly) happily tried out material new and old—and proved that it worked. Thanks to you all.

I'm grateful to my wonderful principal, Mamie Oatis, who kept begging me not to give away all our secrets, was always supportive, and never asked for a cut of the profits for being my agent.

My thanks also go to Don Tutt, who managed to take an author's picture that squeezed Mr. Fitz into the frame with me.

This book wouldn't look as good as it does without the work of Lauren Leon, who took my over-packed manuscript and gigantic art package full of cartoons and managed to fit them gracefully into our page limit with room to spare. Jaime Lucero and Jay Namerow took my suggestion that we might use Mr. Fitz cartoons on the cover and ran with it, and the characters have never looked so good!

Lastly, thanks to anyone who ever told me they liked a comic strip I drew, or who ever clipped one and hung it at their school.

# FOREWORD

• • • • • • • • • • • • • • • • • • • • • • • • • • • • • • • • • • • • • • • • • • • • • • • • •

Most teachers know good writing when they read it and can say with certainty which pieces lie lifeless on their desks and which ones squirm with promise. But after that initial identification, many may not know what to do to help their students improve their writing. If you are one of those teachers (or even if you're not), you hold in your hands a real treasure. This book is absolutely brimming with imaginative, do-able activities you can use with your students today, not generic "strategies" that promise more than they deliver. David provides charts, examples, prompts, and scenarios presented in a fresh, accessible style. And what's more, his original comics will keep you in thoughtful stitches, making you wonder how David came to know your students so intimately. He's been there, no doubt.

*Teaching Students to Make Writing Visual & Vivid* is a celebration of writing, an antidote to the practices spawned by the high-stakes testing culture evident in every school I've visited recently. "Let your students *enjoy* writing," I encourage teachers, who shake their heads in discouragement before my sentence is complete. "No time . . ." they reply in unison. They tell me they feel compelled to have their students write to a prompt, analyze high-scoring papers from previous tests, use words that will "wow" the scorers. Too often, writing has become the means to an end. It's all about the test.

In joyful contrast, David's book is all about the process, the art, the creative magic from which good writing is born. As I read this book (a real page-turner, something I didn't think was possible with professional books), I could *visualize* David's class, his students actively involved in writing, sharing, and revising their pieces. I could sense their amazement as they discovered how mere words can form people, scenes, feelings, and actions that pulse with life. How proud these students must be of their creations! And how fortunate we are that Mr. Fitz has taken time out of his busy, school-filled days to frame a conversation with us about writing.

—ReLeah Cossett Lent, national literacy consultant and author of *Engaging Adolescent Learners*

# INTRODUCTION

**W**ord pictures are the key to good writing. Think about the stories, poems, or essays you remember best. Chances are, you remember pictures you created in your head by collaborating with the author. I can picture Scout on the front porch of Boo Radley's house. I can picture the Highwayman galloping down the road toward the inn at night. I, unfortunately, can picture Jonathan Swift's dinner suggestion in "A Modest Proposal." Most truly effective writing creates pictures in our heads. True, there are exceptions. The Gettysburg Address is a stirring speech that uses little, if any, imagery. The beginning of *A Tale of Two Cities* with its "best of times/worst of times" series of opposites uses a list of adjectives to great effect, but then goes on to tell a story in specific images. I immediately picture a horse-drawn coach stopping in the fog.

Getting our students to create pictures when they write might seem like an easy task. We live in a visual age. Our students are bombarded with images. They watch TV. They buy and rent DVDs. They surf the Internet and watch YouTube. Ironic, then, that when we ask our students to write, many of them immediately write generic stories, essays, and poetry that are all adjectives with few images.

Many student essays will either state that things are "cool" and "great" or pronounce that they are "stupid" or that they "suck." Many student-written stories turn into lists of events. "These two guys stepped off the spaceship, and this alien, it ripped their heads off!" I don't object so much to the violence of a story that reads that way (though it is, I'll admit, appalling). What I really object to is the complete lack of atmosphere, suspense, or imagery! Make me care about the two "guys" so there is something at stake when they get their heads ripped off.

Some students like to tell me that they write poetry because "it's all about their feelings." And sadly, many times that's all they write about—their feelings. I feel sad. I feel happy. I feel bored. They tell you their feelings point blank, but we don't see what is making them feel that way. We can't feel the feelings with them, because adjectives don't create emotions; they merely label them.

And so we are left with a conundrum. Many of our students have a very sophisticated visual sense, but it doesn't translate into words when they write. Many of our students, I suspect, have pictures in their heads, but they are unsure about how to make them appear on the written page. Ironically, the visual age we live in may actually be part of the problem. Unless we read, we are seldom asked to create images in our heads, seldom asked to use our imaginations. When I was a kid, when songs would come on the radio, I would create interesting pictures, sometimes very strange pictures, of the lyrics in my head. When Elton John sang "Crocodile Rock," I could see the characters "holding hands and skimming stones," but they were doing it on Saratoga Lake, near my house in upstate New York. When I heard Billy Joel's "Piano Man," I had images of all the characters in the bar—Davey who was still in the Navy and all the rest. But when I was in high school, MTV appeared, and then it became very hard to visualize songs, because the videographers had done it for you.

But it isn't just music videos doing our visualizing for us. Play used to be more imaginative—making up stories and pretending your backyard was Mars, or a jungle, or secret spy headquarters. Now many children play with toys that do all the work for you—especially video games.

A recent National Public Radio Morning Edition story confirmed this phenomenon for me. "Old Fashioned Play Builds Serious Skills," reported by Alix Spiegel, talks about the shift in play from the nineteenth century, when childhood play was about the *activity* and usually involved a lot of imagination, to the twentieth century, when play became all about the toy. Imaginative play has all kinds of benefits—children learn to regulate their own behavior; they get more exercise; they learn social skills; and, obviously, it helps them develop strong imaginations.

Increasingly, though, we do all the visualizing work *for* children. Why imagine the cardboard box is a house when you can buy a plastic playhouse with working windows, doors, and running water at Toys "R" Us? Why imagine your bike is a spaceship when you can fly a realistic-looking spaceship through simulated space on your computer screen? As a former child Lego junky, I was thrilled at first when Lego introduced *Star Wars* Legos. I'm a complete *Star Wars* junky as well, so it seemed like toy Nirvana. My son was just the right age, so I could buy them for . . . *him*. As I thought about it, though, I realized the irony at work. The chief virtue of the original Legos was that they were just bricks—you had to use your imagination to create your own toys. By making *Star Wars* Legos, the toy makers have done all the work for the children. Now kids don't have to create—they just build. Imagination has taken a beating.

So the situation is complicated. Our students take in visual information well, but many of them are not so good at visualizing things for themselves. And even if they can create mental images, they often have trouble translating those images into words. They view creating pictures as a chore, yet creating pictures is absolutely essential to their success as writers.

When I teach my students to create word pictures, I keep in mind that it is, at heart, a kind of imaginative play—something they may not have done very often. Don't think of imagination as a soft, right-brained, touchy-feely kind of concept. Adults have a tendency to distrust imagination. We will call a story "imaginative" when it contains a lot of strange elements but doesn't make a lot of sense. "That's a nice story about the clown and the killer whale and the talking teapot! It's so imaginative!" But imagination, used properly, is not a loosey-goosey, anything-goes proposition. Imaginative books like the Harry Potter series and *The Lord of the Rings* work precisely because the authors used their imaginations to create internal logic and consistency in their fantasy worlds.

I think about the Imagineers at Walt Disney World, who have to take the most way-out ideas (a train ride through Mount Everest with a Yeti!) and turn them into practical realities. How will we fit this ride into a building this size, with this budget, and where will we put the emergency exits?

So imagination is an odd combination of free-thinking and practicality—not just thinking up ideas, but thinking up the *right* ideas. Students need not only to create pictures, but also to create pictures that fit their purpose, fit their genre, and fit into the flow of the writing. And they need to draw these images with clear, engaging words.

They also need to understand that details aren't "fluff"—an additive to make writing cuter or more "razzle-dazzly." The following strips are based loosely on a real conversation in one of my eighth-grade classes.

Details are, instead, something essential to writing—the very essence of it. That idea, that writing is not fluff or a frill, will be visited frequently throughout the book.

Creating good word pictures is also a skill you get better at with practice—like drawing pictures with lines. The fact that pictures can improve with time is illustrated throughout the pages of this book; as I revised it, I added dozens of cartoons from my Daytona Beach *News-Journal* comic strip "Mr. Fitz." The early strips, from 2000–2001, sometimes make me cringe—they were pretty primitive. Even without checking out the tiny date between the frames on a given strip, you can almost peg which year it came from, 2000 to 2009, based on the quality of the drawings. I think that the most-current strips look a lot better than the early ones. Improvement comes with practice—and that goes for our students' writing as well. Most of the activities and assignments here are designed to give them practice, rather than serve as ends in themselves. Consider them sketches to get your writers ready to create masterpieces.

An important word of explanation: this book is full of what I'm calling *exercises*—short, pointed writing assignments that build specific writing "muscles." These exercises will often be presented as single sentences designed to get students writing in a particular way. As my editor has pointed out to me, a sentence, taken alone, is not an exercise; a writing exercise includes the instruction that comes before the writing, and the feedback that follows. Some of the activities in this book, such as "The Suspect," have the instruction and feedback built into the activity itself. Many of the exercises, though, might at first glance appear to be mere sentences. Here is what typically happens in my classroom that transforms these mere *sentences* into *exercises*.

Before writing, we read and discuss samples of the type of writing we are trying to work on. I will sometimes model the writing skill myself. We also do some brainstorming activities—gathering possible details and types of details.

As students write, I circulate to see if anyone is having difficulty getting started or completing the assignment, and try to help them.

After students write, I nearly always have them exchange papers with someone they know and trust in the class to do a "pair/share" and give each other some kind of specific feedback. I circulate and listen in on these sessions, and give some feedback of my own when I feel it's appropriate. I then give some students the opportunity to share their paragraphs aloud with the class. I ask the other students to count details and offer feedback on which details were the most vivid.

The pattern is this: students read models of good writing, see writing modeled in class, write, and then receive feedback from peers and from the teacher. You will actually see Mr. Fitz modeling some of this process in the comic strips.

The last thing I want students to understand is that writing using pictures doesn't just make writing better. Using word pictures makes writing more *fun*. My hope is that by using the ideas in this book, your students will be able to feel completely engaged as they create pictures with words. Instead of sitting slumped at their desks, listlessly writing to get it over with, imagine your students hunched intently over their papers or keyboards, creating images out of words with intensity and a sense of play. Imagine your students reading each other's papers and reacting to the images they have beamed into each other's heads like magic.

Can you picture that?

# CHAPTER 1

# Pictures Drawn Out of Words: Reading Like a Writer

I have always seen a strong relationship between words and pictures, perhaps because of my very early interest in comic strips, which are a combination of both. I learned to read when I was five or six for a very practical reason—so I could read the newspaper funnies (especially *Peanuts*) without having to beg my older brothers to read them to me. I remember lying on our living room carpet with the funnies stretched out before me and independently reading my first *Peanuts* plotline, which involved Linus and Sally going on a field trip to an actual field, Linus getting stuck on a barn roof, and Snoopy turning into a helicopter to rescue him. After learning to read, I kept on reading the funnies but added books without pictures to my repertoire. What I learned, without really being conscious of the lesson, is that books without pictures *did* have pictures—pictures I drew in my head.

I was recently in The Family Book Shop (one of my local haunts here in DeLand, Florida), buying a few books for my classroom library, when I found a copy of Lloyd Alexander's *The Marvelous Misadventures of Sebastian*. I had not seen this book for many years, but immediately recognized the title. It was one of the first, if not *the* first, chapter books I ever read. I opened it and began looking for the illustrations I remembered of Sebastian's marvelous misadventures. There were no pictures. I had created the pictures. But the impression I'd had all these years was that the book had come with illustrations.

I'm not sure when I first became really, truly conscious of authors creating pictures with words, but it may have been when I read *The Chronicles of Narnia* on my own for the first time. The images in the Narnia books were so striking to me, so vivid, even when they were descriptions of things that would be impossible to find in the real world, that they have stayed with me ever since. I can imagine those settings, those characters, and even the sounds and smells of Narnia as well as I can imagine some places out of my own past. The recent movie versions seemed superfluous to me—I already had in my head a 3-D movie with smell-o-vision and quadraphonic sound.

The pictures of Narnia I created in my head were only the beginning. Nearly every book I can remember reading since, I remember as images in my head. What I discovered as an older reader in high school and college was that nonfiction could create images, too, images that could help you think about life in a different way.

If we want our students to create pictures when they write, we must first make them aware of the pictures in what they are reading. If they are unaware of word pictures, or worse yet, unable to create mental pictures as they read, they will almost certainly fail to write in a way that creates pictures in their readers' heads.

For many of our students, reading is a chore, and visualizing is yet one more chore added to the already mundane work of reading. Other students come to us as avid readers who visualize very well, but even they may be unaware of what writers do to create the pictures they see in their heads as they read. Some combinations of words create pictures in our heads; some combinations of words create no pictures. If we are going to teach young writers how to do the former with their writing, we need to get them visualizing as they read, and then looking at how authors created those images.

What follows for the rest of this chapter is a series of strategies that help students pull images from what they read and analyze how those images were created. Once those skills are in place, getting students to write in word pictures is possible. The added benefit is that reading for details in this way will not only make them better writers, it also helps make them stronger readers.

# Drawing From Text

We want students to create pictures in their heads when they read, but the problem is that the act of visualizing, like much of the reading process, is invisible. Our job is to make visualization visible.

There is a way to make students' visualizations visible, however, and that is to ask them to draw them. Roger Essley's (with Linda Rief and Amy Rocci) *Visual Tools for Differentiating Reading and Writing Instruction* (2008) is devoted to the subject of using drawings to help students read and write better. I will mention some of his techniques for storyboarding, but I will also discuss other ways that drawing can be used to make students' mental images visible.

## Drawing From Narratives

Narratives naturally lend themselves to drawing pictures because a story is a series of concrete events—first this happens, then that, then the other thing—so I often begin teaching visualization with this form of writing. I may start with familiar stories such as the fairy tales I use with my sixth graders, then move to fictional stories from our literature book, and later to narrative essays to bridge the gap between narratives and essays. A great source of narrative essays is the *Reader's Digest* annual edition of "Everyday Heroes." (You can also find recent hero stories online at http://www.rd.com/heroes-stories-of-bravery.) The stories are brief, interesting, and often action-packed. Any of these selections, from fairy tales to "Everyday Heroes" essays, can be used to teach students to create pictures as they read.

### Storyboards

Storyboards are primarily used in the movie business to create a flexible visual script of a movie as it is being planned. Each shot of a movie is rendered as a drawing on a card that indicates the type of shot being planned (e.g., close-up) with sound effects and dialogue noted below the drawing. These cards are placed in order on bulletin boards all around the room, and the creative team discusses how the movie flows and works before ever filming it. Sections can be cut or re-ordered simply by moving, removing, or adding cards.

In our version we are not creating an actual movie necessarily, though that is not out of the question. Instead, we are attempting to re-create on paper the movies students have already created in their heads, or to assist them in producing their own mental movies. This technique works best for narratives, though as we'll see below, it can be adapted for other types of text. You can have students storyboard an entire story, as I often have students do for tales like Rudyard Kipling's "Rikki-tiki-tavi," but you can also take one particular set of events and storyboard them.

Roger Essley makes it clear to students that "bad drawing is fine" (p. 9) in storyboarding and recommends using stick figures for clarity of expression. Although stick figures can be highly effective, I also tell my more artistic students that if they want to cut loose and show off a little, that's okay, too. As a student, I loved to draw (I still do), and if the teacher allowed us to draw, I wanted to use my abilities.

### Full-Story Storyboard

If a narrative isn't too long, I may have my students storyboard the full narrative. This process requires that they not only figure out where the word pictures are, but also which word pictures are important events worth putting on their storyboards. Fairy tales are ideal for this activity, and if you think that sounds too "babyish," try finding the original Grimm's Fairy Tales either online or in print. They are indeed grim—and gory. The students love it. "Cinderella," for instance, is not the prettified Disney version. The stepsisters mutilate their feet to make the slipper fit, and then get blinded by vengeful birds at the wedding. Fun stuff!

I have found that for neatness and clarity it's often good to give students a template or "frames" for their storyboards. I try to fit six to eight frames on a page. I usually model a storyboard for the class based on a very short, very simple story such as "The Three Little Pigs." Picking out the main events is simple, and drawing the events with "stick pigs" and a "stick wolf" takes hardly any time at all. You are teaching students to summarize the main events by drawing storyboards this way. Many teachers do this kind of summarizing, but we don't very often point out to students that we are able to draw (in both senses of the word) pictures out of the story only because the story used words to create pictures.

"The Three Little Pigs," written as a plot summary, creates few pictures at all.

*Once there were three pigs. They went and built three places to live. A wolf came and ate the first two but then got killed by the last pig.*

The details the author adds to that bare-bones plot are what create the pictures. When I discuss the way authors write narratives, I begin to use the terms "list-of-events narration" and "moment-by-moment narration." A plot summary lists events without much detail— a list-of-events narration—and some students write their stories that way. A narrative creates pictures because it goes into moment-by-

1-1: Student artwork "draws out" the main events of a familiar story.

moment narration to tell us, in detail, what the characters are doing. This distinction becomes important whenever students write narratives, either fiction or nonfiction.

## Plot Storyboard

Another storyboard template I've developed does double duty; it not only gets students to visualize on paper, but it also gets them to analyze for plot structure. Designed around the Freytag Pyramid, this template gives students a way to draw the main events in terms of Exposition, Climax, Rising and Falling Action, and Resolution. A blank version of the plot storyboard can be found in Appendix D, page 140.

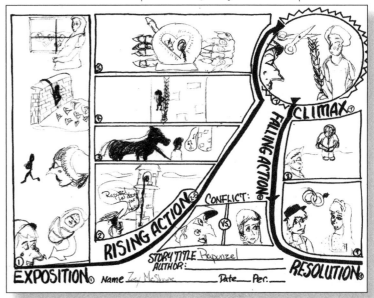

1-2: A sixth grader's storyboard of the fairy tale "Rapunzel" creates a visual map of the story's major events and plot structure.

I tell students that when they put their pictures in, they should actually do so out of order. They should start with the exposition square, which is easy since it always represents the beginning of the story, then draw the resolution, which is also easy because it always comes at the end. Next they should pick out which event is the climax of the story and draw that, because the rising and falling action are framed by those other three parts of the story. The climax, of course, is the turning point for the main character, or the high point of the action (or both) right near the end of the story. Once the climax is drawn in, then they fill in four events from the rising action and one picture for a brief falling action.

I ask them to think that way—deciding on beginning, ending, and turning point first— because many fiction writers actually think that way when they write. They have the beginning and end in mind before they write, and then decide what the climax of the story will be. Only then do they design the action to lead to that ending. They begin with the end of the story in mind rather than just making it up as they go, as most students prefer to do. We talk about the Harry Potter books and how J. K. Rowling had the whole series, and each book, planned out before she started writing.

This may be a little advanced for some students, but I have found it helps them to see the story structure in a much more vivid way than simply listing the events in words.

## Event Storyboard

Sometimes if a story is longer, and creating a storyboard of the whole plot would be too complex, I will ask students to create a storyboard of just one event of the story—especially if it's a story with a lot of action. I will sometimes read through the text myself and either draw it or count out how many individual pictures it would take to re-create the event as a storyboard. I'll then give the students an estimate of how many drawings they will need to create their storyboards.

One scene that can be used to great effect for an event storyboard is from "The Rule of Names," a story by Ursula K. Le-Guin, set in her fantasy world of Earthsea. Its climax is a wizard's duel between Mr. Blackbeard, who is seeking his lost family treasure, and Mr. Underhill, who stole it. As they duel, they transform themselves into different creatures and forces of nature. This scene usually results in some spectacular drawings, and students have a great time reading it and drawing it. As part of an inquiry unit on happiness, I

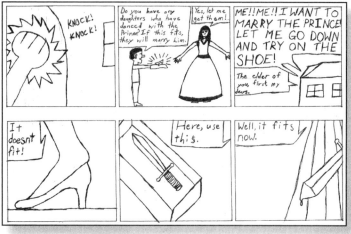

1-3: A sixth grader's event storyboard of a rather gory event from the original Grimm's Brothers "Cinderella" uses comic strip techniques and cinematic framing and camera angles.

have also had students draw scenes from the original, grim Grimm's fairy tales. Figure 1-3 is one student's depiction of a stepsister sacrificing her heel to make the slipper fit.

Another story that lends itself to a moment-by-moment storyboard is "Up the Slide" by Jack London. This story is actually quite challenging for students to visualize, and they may need a lot of assistance. A young man in the Yukon, Clay, wants to get a dead pine tree from a crevice in a cliff face so he can sell it for firewood. What seems like a simple endeavor—climb up to the tree, knock it down, climb back down—soon becomes a nightmare when getting down turns into a life-threatening proposition. He winds up going down, then up again, then sliding down by accident, and then climbing all the way back up again. A careful reading of the text is necessary to visualize the setting and the events involved. We sometimes read through the story together, visualizing and drawing together as a class as we read, because if you aren't visualizing the story, you simply aren't reading it at all.

## Pictures of Settings

Another technique I use with "Up the Slide" that is vital to understanding the story is not only to draw close-ups of the events themselves but also to depict the whole setting: the river, the cliff face, the gully or "slide," the pine tree, the gorge at the top of the slide, and the grove of pine trees Clay finds beyond it.

The chapter "A Boy and a Man" from James Ramsey Ullman's *Banner in the Sky* (1988) creates an interesting situation to visualize. Rudy, the 16-year-old protagonist, finds that he must rescue a climber who is trapped on a ledge down a crevasse in a glacier. The third-person limited narration does not directly describe the situation. We get it described in pieces, part description from Rudy's point of view, part dialogue as the trapped man describes his predicament. A clear picture emerges of the man's situation and what Rudy must do to rescue him. Asking students to draw a picture of the situation does not require a great deal of drawing talent, but it does require that they understand the text itself.

In any story where a setting is important, I will frequently ask students to draw a picture, map, or floor plan of the setting. I ask students to draw a map or floor plan if the position of geographical features, rooms, or objects is vital to the story.

## Floor Plans

One story that lends itself to a floor plan is James Thurber's "The Night the Bed Fell" (which also lends itself to a great storyboard). Thurber actually describes the layout of the bedrooms in his childhood home, and that layout becomes central to the action of the story.

A floor plan is even more vital to the story "The Adventure of the Speckled Band," Sir Arthur Conan Doyle's Sherlock Holmes mystery about a murder and attempted murder in an old mansion. The rooms are described in detail, and drawing floor plans helps students not only visualize but also make predictions about how the murder was committed.

## Maps of Settings

I have a special fondness for books with maps. I still treasure the memory of my first reading of *The Lord of the Rings* because the library edition I read had a large fold-out map in the back cover. When I was in ninth grade, my project for *To Kill a Mockingbird* was a map of the town, Maycomb. I remember being very careful to draw it in such a way that the view from the Radley front porch would allow for a view of all the major events of the story—an important point at the end of the book.

Any story that is set outside the confines of a house is a great opportunity to draw a map, and stories that take characters on journeys are even better. And again, drawing a map requires a detailed understanding of the story. Does the map hold up when compared to the actual text? Drawing a map also requires that students pay attention to how the author described the setting. Not only the various elements of the setting but also their relationships to each other must be visualized. How does the author reveal the setting? Through the eyes of a character? Through dialogue? Most students don't read to see what an author actually does so they can apply it to their own

1-4: Creating this drawing helped a student visualize the predicament of a fallen mountain climber in "A Boy and a Man."

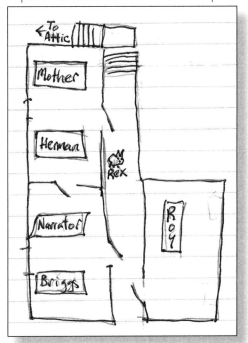

1-5: This student used a description from James Thurber's "The Night the Bed Fell" to create a floor plan of the house where the action takes place.

writing. Having them draw pictures of characters and settings requires a different kind of reading, in which students not only take in the details on the page but also note and appreciate how they were written.

## Pictures of Characters

Rather than illustrating events or settings, students can also illustrate people from text—either characters in fiction or real people in nonfiction. If you want your students to be aware of how authors describe characters' physical appearances, then asking them to draw characters based on the descriptions from books is a terrific way to do it.

The challenge, of course, is to find specific descriptions of characters. This can be harder than it sounds. Pick up a random young adult novel, and skim through the first few pages to find a description. What you'll discover is that authors describe characters different ways—some characters and people are drawn in great detail, while others are delivered in very broad strokes. If you have a lot of details in the text, the character is easier to draw; if the description is more general, you have to create details from your imagination that fit the overall "feel" of the character.

This can lead to a discussion about character descriptions and the way authors write them. How much detail is enough to create a picture of the character in your head? How much detail becomes overwhelming? How does an author choose the most important details?

These matters will be discussed in a later chapter—for now it's enough to say that drawing pictures of characters is an excellent way to practice visualization, and to become aware of how authors describe people.

# Drawing From Essays—Concrete Narrative vs. Abstract Essay

Of course, some students create great pictures if they are writing narratives but go completely blank when they begin to write an expository or persuasive essay. As I was drafting this chapter, I was dealing with students who didn't understand the difference between a narrative and an essay. They wanted to turn everything they wrote into a narrative. I had to explain that narratives tell a story and are "concrete," but that essays are built around a series of abstract ideas. It is not event, event, event in most essays; it is reasons, reasons, reasons, or examples, examples, examples. As an essay writer you are "fleshing out" abstract ideas. Pictures don't happen as naturally in essays as they do in narratives, but despite that, or maybe because of it, effective imagery is even more important. An essay without word pictures leaves nothing in the mind to remember it by—abstractions are made of Teflon. As Steven Pinker writes in *The Stuff of Thought*, ". . . even our most abstract concepts are understood in terms of concrete scenarios" (p. 3).

### Picture Outline

The picture outline, a kind of modified Cornell note-taking, is something I developed to help students see the flow of main ideas—the abstractions—in an essay, as well as the word pictures that make those abstractions concrete.

| Main Ideas (Abstractions) | Word Pictures (Concrete images as drawings) |
|---|---|
| | |

The left-hand column is for the main ideas; the right-hand column is a place to represent the pictures with stick figure storyboard drawings.

The chart in Figure 1-6 analyzes Brad Meltzer's essay "Why I Love Superman."

When I introduce this method for reading an essay, the class reads the essay aloud together, discussing the main ideas as we go, as I draw the chart on my dry-erase board. After we have done a couple of essays together, I ask them to create picture outlines in pairs, and then on their own with new essays. Doing an outline this way has several advantages. The "abstractions" column reinforces the idea of pulling the "main ideas" out of the different paragraphs. It also allows students to see the flow of ideas and to discuss how those ideas are ordered—which is seldom done as a five-paragraph formula essay. Students are amazed to see how often writers save the main idea of the whole essay for the conclusion. The right-hand column is enjoyable because they are able to draw, but it also makes visible the idea of creating concrete word pictures.

1-6: Nick's T-chart plots the main ideas (left) and word pictures (right) of the essay "Why I Love Superman" and uses doodles to recreate the word pictures.

# Noting the Words That Make Pictures

If your students have already been drawing (in both senses of the word) pictures out of text, and therefore have internalized the fact that good writing creates pictures, you may want them to start noting how the pictures are built with words. If this is the case, a few other graphic organizers to use when reading may show the way.

## Nouns and Verbs

If you are not concerning yourself or your students with the flow of ideas in an essay, then this chart may prove useful. It may prove especially useful, because it can also be utilized as a prewriting tool, as I will describe in the next chapter. The nouns-verbs chart is a simple T-chart like this:

| Concrete Nouns | Strong Verbs |
| --- | --- |
|  |  |

As students read, they simply list the concrete nouns from the essay in the first column and the strong verbs that go with them in the other. If it sounds simple, it is, but it is also powerful because it shows students that creating word pictures is not, at heart, mysterious, complicated,

1-7

or difficult. It is about using specific, concrete objects, and verbs that name actions you can see. Figure 1-7 is a chart from the essay "After the Dishes" by Robert Fulghum.

It becomes hard for students to miss the fact that the essays they are reading contain loads of word pictures; it also becomes hard for them not to notice how most of them are constructed.

## Noun–Verb–Writing Tool Chart

As you begin to teach your students more specific types of visual writing techniques, it may be helpful to ask them to identify not only the nouns and verbs used to create the word pictures, but also the kind of writing "picture tools" the author used. Later in this book we will be looking in depth at those tools (figurative language, anecdote, moment-by-moment narration, and hyperbole). As you introduce these tools to your students, you can have students note their use on the chart.

| Concrete Nouns | Strong Verbs | Writing Tool |
|---|---|---|
|  |  |  |

## Abstractions-Nouns-Verbs Chart

This reading chart is similar to the picture outline above, because it focuses on the abstractions and the flow of ideas, but instead of drawing pictures, students focus again on the nouns and verbs. The advantage of this chart is that it actually enables students to see the differences between abstract words and specific ones, starkly displayed on a chart.

The words in the first column will tend to be abstract and general. The words in the

| Main Ideas (Abstractions) | Concrete Nouns | Strong Verbs |
|---|---|---|
|  |  |  |

columns to the right, the nouns and verbs, should create word pictures of those abstractions. Like the chart with pictures, it serves as a way for students to read for several things at once: the overall flow of ideas, the relationship between the abstract and the specific, and the way nouns and verbs team up to create pictures.

## Highlighting, Marking, and Labeling

If you are all "charted out" by this point, there are other ways to get students noting word pictures. If you have hard copies of an essay that students can mark up (they sometimes come in workbooks, for instance), then asking students to highlight everything that is a word picture is a great way to emphasize how much of an essay should be visual. If that's your goal, you might want to highlight the essay first yourself, to be sure that it is visual. Assuming that it is, highlighting the word pictures is a way to show students how much of a given essay should be devoted to the specific. Students are usually astounded that as much as 80 or 90 percent of a given essay may be highlighted. In other words, with the exception of the main ideas—the abstractions—many essays are highly visual. Students can later use the same technique on their own rough drafts when writing, and when they do, they can use the amount of text highlighted to gauge whether they need to add more detail or not.

Marking the text is also useful, and easier logistically, since it doesn't require you to supply highlighters. Simply have students underline all the word pictures on a hard copy of the text. The effect is the same as with highlighting—they see how much of an essay is visual. An added technique is to have students circle all the strong verbs and underline the concrete nouns. This doesn't necessarily show them how much of the text is visual, but it does point out the specific words that make the text visual.

In addition to marking the text this way, students can also note in the margin which writer's tools are used to create pictures, much as they did on the Noun/Verb/Writing Tool chart on page 18.

## Reading Workshop Sharing

Another way to get students to draw pictures out of texts, and one that requires no charts, no paper, and no grading at all (except maybe some extra credit), is to ask students to find examples of word pictures in their own reading. On Fridays we do Reading Workshop in my class, and one of the things we will share at the end of class is any particularly well-written word pictures we ran into in the books we've been reading.

I may get the ball rolling by mentioning things from the book I am reading (well, one of the books—I'm usually juggling four or five). Once students start sharing, I may ask for specific examples of types of word pictures or writer's tools. Who has a good description of a setting or character? Who has a good example of hyperbole or figurative language? Who has good examples of sensory detail? We can then discuss what made those word pictures particularly good. Were there any particularly effective specific nouns? Any verbs that seemed just right to the situation?

In the following Mr. Fitz strips, I had Mr. Fitz getting Rusty, a reluctant reader, to do what active readers experience when they are immersed in books. An activity like this at the end of Reading Workshop helps tie students' own reading to the kinds of writing we want them to do in class.

## Reading Visually Leads to Writing Visually

Students won't write visually and use word pictures until they're aware of them in the texts they read. And they not only need to be made aware of word pictures, they also need to *appreciate* them. We need them to read word pictures that affect them—make them laugh, shudder, smile—maybe even cry. We need to emphasize that few people have ever been touched, amused, or called to action by an adjective. Only pictures can do those things.

Creating pictures and putting them to use is the focus of the rest of this book.

# Picture Basics: Abstract to Concrete

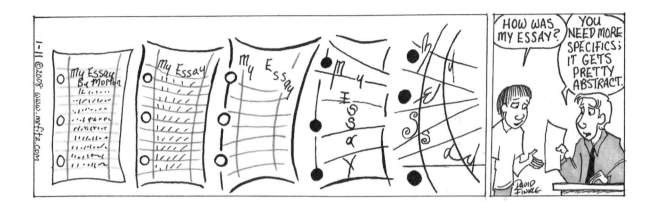

recently began using Facebook, the social networking site. On Facebook, which many of my students are on as well, you can write a "status update" several times a week, day, or hour and keep your "friends" updated on what you are doing nearly constantly if you so desire. Status updates are brief, usually a sentence, yet I find myself drawn to read some more than others—for reasons that have nothing to do with who the friend is, but rather with the quality and entertainment value of the writing itself.

Take a look at these status updates, based on real Facebook updates, but with the details changed. Which ones do you find more interesting?

"Mark is chillin' at home."

"Cindy is happy she got an A on the test."

"Jill is bored."

"Jim just ran a 5K race today and won."

"Angel wonders what she should do with her leftovers—maybe put them on display as modern art."

"Kim ate fried chicken today and can hear herself gaining weight."

Did you rate 4, 5, and 6 as more interesting than 1, 2, and 3? If you showed these updates to your students and asked them to rate them, they would most likely rate them the same way. But what makes the lower group of sentences more engaging than the top half? Part of it is the obvious attempt to be amusing in 5 and 6, but 4 isn't particularly witty, and yet it is still more interesting than 1, 2, or 3. The answer, I think, lies in the types of words being used. Even with something as short and usually trivial as a Facebook status update, certain principles of writing still hold true. What do 1, 2, and 3 share that makes them less interesting? Dead verbs and adjectives. One of the first things I try to teach my students is that adjectives alone do not create pictures. They are the seasoning, but not the main ingredient. What's the main ingredient, the thing that makes 4, 5, and 6 more fun to read? Strong verbs and concrete nouns.

## Strong Verbs and Concrete Nouns

Student writing often operates at the level of a dull, adjective-laden Facebook post. When I asked a group of eighth graders to write an essay about a best friend, they inundated me with a sea of adjectives. I nearly drowned in them, pulled under by tidal waves of *fun, funny, caring, cool, smart, understanding,* and *good.* All the essays sounded alike. I even read excerpts aloud to the class and asked them to guess who wrote them.

Even the authors couldn't identify their own papers. When we rely on adjectives alone in our writing, we don't create any pictures, only abstractions.

Readers don't remember, retain, relate to, or become moved by abstractions. If you tell me your friend is caring, I may nod politely and ask about the weather. If you tell me your friend spent his own birthday money to buy you the new electric guitar you thought you'd never be able to afford, I will sit up, take notice, and maybe sit slack-jawed for a moment before saying, "Wow!"

## Acting Out a Picture: The Teacher Was Angry

My first writing lesson of the year is designed to teach my students to use strong verbs and concrete nouns. I used to try to get whole paragraphs out of students right off the bat, but I've learned in recent years that for beginning writers, even those who have been writing longer pieces earlier in school, it is sometimes good to go back to the basics for a bit. We practice writing some good, strong sentences.

I do this by giving students topic sentences that are "telling," that is, sentences that are adjective- and dead-verb-based, and asking them to transform them. I model the process first with a demonstration. On the board I write the sentence, "The teacher was angry," and we discuss whether that sentence creates a picture in their heads. Many students say it does create a picture in their heads, but upon further examination, we discover that they all have different pictures in their heads, not the pictures I wanted them to have. I haven't done my job as a writer because they all supplied their own pictures by imagining one of their own angry teachers. I then say, "Well, how about this sentence?" and proceed to "perform" the following sentence—rather loudly: "The teacher slammed a dictionary on the floor, tipped over a stool, threw an eraser across the room, and yelled 'I'm not going to take this anymore!'"

After everyone has recovered from the shock of my actually doing those things, we write the sentence on the board and analyze it. We have concrete nouns—*teacher*, *dictionary*, *stool*, and *eraser*—and strong verbs—*slammed*, *tipped*, *threw*, and *yelled*. Those words create pictures, and they are more fun.

This is an important point to make and continue making: writing with pictures is more fun than being vague. It makes your writing better, yes, and will raise your grade—but it is also just more fun to write this way. I emphasize that fact over and over again throughout the year. In some narrative writing exercises I've recently done with my seventh-grade classes, we've been noting how many different reactions you can get out of your audience by using word pictures. My students have had each other laughing uproariously, but also uttering a long, low "Oooooh!" when the writing was particularly suspenseful or touching. My students never have audible reactions to adjectives, but they are quite responsive when a writer says her older brother dragged her down the stairs, clunking her head on every step (a scene that was complete fiction; the student doesn't even have a brother!), or when a student writes about hiding in a bush while some kind of monster passes by inches from her hiding place, exhaling its foul breath and sniffing for her.

After I have demonstrated how to create a word picture using the angry teacher as an example, we write some examples together. I write a telling sentence on the board and the students assist me in rewriting it. Then they write some sentences of their own with my assistance until they get the hang of it.

## "Happiness is . . ." Posters

Another activity I use to get students to see the contrast between the two types of writing, showing and telling, is the "Happiness is. . ." poster. I share with them a recently reissued Peanuts book by Charles Schulz called *Happiness Is a Warm Puppy*. Each two-page spread is a "happiness statement" on one page and an illustration on the other. Happiness is always something specific: a warm puppy, an "A" on a spelling test, lots of flavors of ice cream. We note that these statements have concrete nouns yet lack strong verbs, but that the illustrations of Charlie Brown and the other characters make up for the missing strong verbs.

After I share the book with my students, I ask them to write their own "happiness is" lists. They simply write, "Happiness is. . ." at the top of a page, and then list a lot of specific things that make them happy. For their poster project, I ask them to take their favorite happiness statement and circle it. Then, at the bottom of the page, they take out the "happiness is" phrase and rewrite the statement as a word picture with a strong verb. "Happiness is a cool pool on a hot afternoon" becomes "I ran through the afternoon heat and plunged into the pool."

The poster itself is very simple. At the top, students write their "happiness is" statements; at the bottom, they write their strong verb sentences; in the middle, they draw a picture that illustrates both sentences.

This little project highlights the value of concrete nouns and strong verbs, shows the difference between dead verb and strong verb sentences, and, by asking them to draw, emphasizes that word pictures are so specific that we can actually draw them if we want. I use this project as part of an inquiry unit about what makes us happy (a more complicated issue than it might seem at first).

2-1

Happiness is pizza!

I devoured my steaming hot pizza until I couldn't fit another morsel of food into my stomach.

-Kyle Burda

2-2

Happiness is a fuzzy, loving dog.

On three, I jump and lick his face.

Cookie wags her tail, jumps on me with her fuzzy body, and licks my face.

From the idea of doing very focused work on word pictures, one sentence at a time, came the idea to do a school-wide writing contest—the Picture This! Contest.

# The Picture This! School-Wide Contest

I kicked around the idea of the Picture This! Contest for several months before finally acting on it. I think my excuse was that I couldn't find a shoe box. But I finally got a new pair of running shoes and no longer had a choice. I covered the box with white paper and put a slot in the lid, a pouch on the front for entry forms, and a sign sticking up out of the back to display the week's topic.

Once the box was set up, I created a list of "telling" topic sentences. My basic principles in writing these sentences are that each sentence must use a dead verb and an adjective, but they must also be specific enough to lend themselves to elaboration. At one point I asked students for topic sentences, but many were unusable because they were completely vague. "It was fun." "It was cool." "We had a lousy time." Sentences like that just don't seem to lead anywhere in particular. I try to include at least one specific noun, either an object or location, for students to focus on. The following list of contest sentences is one that I add to frequently. It's an expansion of the list from *Writing Extraordinary Essays* (Finkle, 2008).

## "Telling" Sentences for Picture This!

The room was messy.
The car was a piece of junk.
The hallway was crowded.
The storm was scary.
My friend makes me laugh.
The sunrise was beautiful.
I had a bad cold.
I laughed really hard.
The old house looked creepy.
It was a bad meal.
It was a good book.
The party was wild.
The lake was ice cold.
The traffic jam went on for miles.
The Buffalo wings were really hot.
I was really sleepy.
The roller coaster was scary.
The cotton candy was messy.
The backpack was overloaded.
The kitchen was filthy.
The suitcase was really heavy.
We had fun at the fair.

The first day of school was really hectic.
The teacher was boring.
The cafeteria was a mess.
The tree was perfect for climbing.
The old computer was very, very slow.
She/he was wearing a really ugly sweater.
The substitute was angry.
His sneakers were very old.
It was a gloomy day.
The Thanksgiving table overflowed with food.
The locker was about to burst.
It was very windy out.
He was clumsy.
The road was bumpy.
The hill was really steep.
I ran as fast as I could.
The party was a flop.
The new entertainment center was gigantic.
The coffee table was cluttered.
He/She was driving me subtly, quietly crazy all through class.

After posting the new topic on the box and placing the box in our Media Center, I have the topic announced on the news. I wait a week or two for entries to roll in. Some come from individual students entering, but some teachers at our school have all their students write entries and then send me the best of them to be considered as finalists. It doesn't take long to sort through the entries and identify the "keepers." My criteria are simple: Does it create a picture? Is it not too "over the top"? Is it mostly grammatically correct? Is it original, and does it avoid clichés?

After the nonsensical and incoherent clunkers are eliminated, I whittle the keepers down to the best three to four—those with the strongest verbs, concrete nouns, and memorable imagery—and pick them as the winners. The winners' names are announced on the school television news, they receive a little prize bag, and the winning sentences run on the "scroll" on the school television station all day until the next winners are announced.

I also have my cartooning club make actual pictures based on the winning word pictures, and these are laminated and hung in various locations around the school. Some examples appear below.

This contest accomplishes a couple of things. It raises awareness of the idea of creating word pictures in your writing. It gives students two ways to be published—on the school television station and around the school on posters like the ones at right. The winners also serve as examples for the rest of the school, even for students who never enter the contest. I sometimes use the winners in class as examples of word pictures. Organizing the Picture This! Contest is a relatively small investment of my time that has any number of payoffs, and I am still finding ways to use it.

2-3: "Picture This" contest winners: the original contest sentence at the top, the winning "word picture" sentence at the bottom, and another student's drawing of the winning sentence in the middle

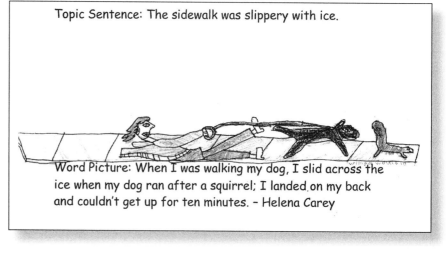

# The Nouns-Verbs Chart

Another technique I use in class, whether we are doing short writing exercises or longer, finished pieces, is the nouns-verbs chart. This very simple chart is a great thing to use to get beginning writers started and to give more-advanced writers a review of the fundamentals. The chart looks like this, and students can use their own sheets of paper to make their own charts—it takes only seconds!

This chart is a prewriting technique. Once you've given students a topic, or they've chosen one of their own, they do a quick brainstorm—how many concrete nouns can they think of that they would associate with their topic? How many strong verbs? For instance, I might give students a topic sentence such as "The roller coaster was scary," and then give them about three minutes to brainstorm (either in pairs or by themselves) concrete nouns they associate with the topic. They are not worried about classifying the nouns at this point—some may refer to the roller coaster itself, some to the rider.

2-4

| Concrete Nouns | Strong Verbs |
| --- | --- |
| track | |
| car | |
| wheels | |
| stomach | |
| heart | |
| hair | |
| drops | |
| turns | |
| loops | |
| twists | |
| eyes | |
| arms | |
| voice | |
| knuckles | |
| upchuck | |
| safety bar | |
| seat | |
| sky | |

After sharing and listing some of the students' words on the board, then discussing them, we switch modes, and they brainstorm strong verbs this time. These verbs might relate directly to the nouns they just listed, but they might also be "freestanding." And like the nouns, they could refer to the roller coaster rider, the coaster itself, or any object related to the experience that can have a verb applied to it.

With even half of these words at their disposal, it would be hard not to write a paragraph that vividly depicted a scary roller coaster.

Once students begin to write with pictures out of sheer habit, this activity may become obsolete, but sometimes it isn't bad to revisit it, even with experienced writers.

2-4

| Concrete Nouns | Strong Verbs |
| --- | --- |
| track | shook, rattled |
| car | plunged, climbed, dropped, plummeted, flew |
| wheels | wobbled, turned, roared |
| stomach | lurched, churned, turned, gurgled |
| heart | pounded, thudded |
| hair | flew, waved, flapped |
| drops | spiraled, fell |
| turns | hugged |
| loops | circled |
| twists | barrelled, hugged, spun |
| eyes | popped, bulged, squeezed shut |
| arms | flailed, waved, clutched |
| voice | screamed, whimpered, yelled, whooped |
| knuckles | turned (white) |
| upchuck | gagged, puked, barfed |
| safety bar | lowered |
| seat | bounced |
| sky | rolled, reversed places |

*Chapter 2: Picture Basics: Abstract to Concrete*

# Adjectives (and Dead Verbs) Are Additives

Sometimes students can get very legalistic about the idea of using strong verbs and concrete nouns. They see published authors overusing adjectives and relying on dead verbs, and they start to criticize them; they see their fellow students using them, and they start to tear apart their peers' papers in writing conferences.

To avoid this, I point out to students that some use of dead verbs and adjectives is okay. Adjectives, I tell them, are like the seasoning in cooking; strong verbs and concrete nouns are the main ingredients. You can't create a dish with just seasoning, but you can spice one up with it. Once we've established the principle that nouns and verbs create pictures, we talk about how adjectives and adverbs add a touch more color to those pictures. We start to note when and where authors use them, and to collect interesting adjectives. As for dead verbs, to use *was* or *is* in a topic sentence is perfectly okay. And even in the body of a paper, some sentences just sound awkward without the dead verb.

I tried for a week to not use the dead verb *is* in my Facebook status update. It . . . *is* difficult. If you can cut dead verbs, it's great to do so, but not if you come off sounding stilted. The guideline I give my students now is to avoid using dead verbs as much as you can, but if you must use them, at least link them to a strong verb instead of an adjective. Then you are still creating pictures.

That last sentence in the previous paragraph is a case in point. It uses the dead verb "are." But if I write it, "Then you still create pictures," it doesn't quite flow. Using the dead verb is okay, though, because I still have the stronger verb *create* there.

The point isn't to create a set of limiting rules about the kinds of words to use, but to create a set of guiding principles. If I had to list them, they would look like this:

1. Good writing is all about the pictures you create.

2. Nouns and verbs are the key ingredients to creating word pictures.

3. Dead verbs do not create pictures and should be used sparingly.

4. Adjectives and adverbs are seasoning, not the key ingredients.

Different cooks may play around with how they mix the ingredients, but no cook worth her salt makes a meal primarily out of . . . salt. However, to extend my already overtaxed food metaphor just a little further, there are many different dishes you can make with a few basic ingredients.

# CHAPTER 3

# Pictures That Make Sense (and Scents): Sensory Details

In a later chapter I'll be discussing how words can create movies, but in this chapter I'll focus on how words can outdo movies every time. Most movies cannot go beyond the senses of sight and sound. Unless we're in some theme-park interactive movie experience, movies will not give us smell, taste, or physical sensation. Words, unlike movies, can help us delve into all five senses—but it isn't easy. There are particular pitfalls that come with sensory detail, but there are also incredible payoffs if you can do it well.

I will not focus in this chapter on the sense of sight, since so much of the rest of this book is about that sense. I will instead focus mainly on the other four senses: sound, smell, taste, and touch.

## The Pitfalls of Sensory Details

Using sensory detail in writing is a good thing, but it must be used well or it can stop a story or essay in its tracks. One of the most common problems in writing classes is some students' over-eagerness to please us teachers. They hear us say, "Use the five senses," and in an attempt to prove to us that they are doing exactly what we ask, they proceed to hit us over the head with sensory detail.

They write things like, "With my NOSE I could SMELL the yummy pancakes," and, "With my EARS I could HEAR the bacon sizzling in the pan," and "With my MOUTH I could TASTE the yummy breakfast at my grandma's house." Unsubtle, to say the least.

Some teachers overcompensate by asking students to avoid using not only the sensory organs by name but also sense words such as *smelled*, *heard*, *felt*, or *tasted*. This constraint makes using the senses nearly impossible. So what are we, and our student writers, to do? Once again, it's time to pay a visit to some professional writers.

## Senses in Books

I often ask my students to find examples of sensory sentences or passages in the books they are reading and share them with the class. Until we take them out of context and look at what writers actually do, we may be giving students misinformed advice, such as "Don't use the sense words." In fact, my advice not to mention the sense *organs* is sometimes wrong, as well. It isn't *which* words you use when dealing with the senses that matters; it's *how* you use them. In the following examples, the emphasis on the sensory words is mine.

In one suspenseful scene in Carl Hiaasen's young adult novel *Scat*, the author uses sense words in close succession. "Nick killed the flashlight. He could *sense* Marta trembling at his side. In the smothering blackness, he reached out and found one of her hands. She squeezed back fiercely. By now they could *hear* the cadence of human breathing outside the steamer trunk . . ." (p. 140).

In *Harry Potter and the Prisoner of Azkaban*, when a werewolf is running away, J. K. Rowling writes that "the *sound* of his paws faded into silence as he pounded away across the grounds." In *The Book of Three*, by Lloyd Alexander, the hero, Taran, is struggling through a tunnel to escape a castle, followed by Eilonwy, a princess he has just sort-of rescued. "Behind him, he *heard* Eilonwy gasping and struggling." (p. 71). Obviously, "Don't use sense words" is not a written–in-stone writers' law, never to be broken.

Smell can be especially difficult to write about without using words like *smell* (either as a noun or a verb), *odor*, *aroma*, or *stench*. In my young adult novel *Making My Escape*, I wrote that the father's mechanic's garage "was always dark and damp and *smelled* of oil and stale beer." (p. 16) It's a detail readers remember, but I used the sense word to create it.

Although using sense words is not forbidden, I challenge students to find passages where the sense is used, but not the sense word. Also in *Making My Escape*, I use sounds to make the protagonist's yet-to-be-seen father seem sinister. Daniel is in his room and hears his father's truck outside. "The engine sputtered and died out and the chains stopped swinging. The door opened with a loud creak, and its slam shut echoed across the yard. His boots crunched on the gravel, were silenced on the grass as he stopped and lit a cigarette, and thumped across the blacktop of the driveway" (p. 30).

Of course, getting students to listen, much less be sensitive to sounds, can be a challenge.

## Sensory Options

In the end, it isn't so much rules as options that matter when using sensory detail. If you review published examples with your students, you will find quite a few different ways of using sensory detail. What follows is a list of sensory methods gleaned from our reading in my class.

### Mention the Sense

As we saw in the examples above from published works, this technique is not as bad an idea as some writing mavens would have you think. Depending on the situation, there is nothing wrong with saying things like *I heard, I smelled, I tasted, I felt, I saw*. Too many of these words used in quick succession might get tiresome, but in some situations simply using the sense word is the easiest, most graceful way to create a memorable sensory image. Trying to avoid the sense word sometimes becomes more awkward than simply using it.

### Personal Effects

Another sometimes looked-down-on method for using the senses is to mention the sense organs. But again, writing about how a sensory phenomenon affects your body is sometimes very vivid.

Saying that a light made you squint and tear up is better than noting that the light was bright. A noise that makes your ears ring or causes you to plug them is probably loud. Cupping your hand around your ear and tilting your head can show us that you are listening to some quiet, far-off sound. Wrinkling or plugging your nose and curling your lip probably indicate that the smell you are experiencing is less than fragrant. Shoveling food into your mouth might indicate that something tastes good—or that you're a boor. Mentioning how a person is reacting to a stimulus tells us a lot about the stimulus itself (and sometimes reflects on the person or character).

## Direct Sensory Input—For Sound and Touch

Sometimes when you write, the action of a person or object indicates the sensation that is being perceived.

| Sense | Example |
|---|---|
| Hearing | *Cedric cleared his throat.* |
| Hearing | *The door slammed.* |
| Touch | *The cool breeze ruffled his hair and pushed him backwards.* |
| Touch | *The heat filled every inch of the house, closing in on him.* |

Notice that with direct sensory input, no explicit sense word is needed. A person (Cedric) or an object (the door) does something that makes a noise. A sensory phenomenon like a cold breeze or heat actually does something (ruffles, pushes, fills, or closes in). Note that it is sensory detail without sense words. This method works equally well with sound and touch. Taste and smell are another matter.

## Action Senses—Smell, Taste, Sound, and Touch

Try rephrasing the following descriptions without using any kind of "sense" word like *smell* or *taste* (or synonyms of them).

*The aroma of apple pie wafted through the kitchen.*
*The doughy-sweet, soft-crisp flavor of hot apple pie filled my mouth.*

It is virtually impossible to describe smell and taste without using words for smell and taste, at least so far as I've been able to discover. I've attempted to either find or create examples of sentences that describe them without sense words, and so far I've been unsuccessful. I think the problem lies in the fact that when you discuss sound, sight, or touch, you can talk about the objects themselves doing things. *The door slammed* creates sound without using the word *sound*. *Slammed* is an action with a built-in sound. There are no actions with built-in smells or tastes. You nearly always have to mention smell and taste directly if you are going to talk about them at all, but there are creative ways to go about mentioning them. Rather than simply saying smells were "good" or "bad," renaming smells and tastes and giving them something to do can, pardon the pun, spice up any sensory description.

### Sense Synonyms

Renaming smells and tastes means hauling out the old thesaurus and looking up some alternate words for *smell* and *taste* as nouns. Smell is a pretty versatile concept. A smell (as a noun) can also be a stench, stink, aroma, odor, scent, fragrance, perfume, or trace. Choosing just the right word for *smell* gives your reader information about the smell itself, or at least how you feel about it. Taste, on the other hand, is a very limited concept. A taste can be a flavor, a savor, or a tang. That's about it. Not a wide range of choices. However, with those two limited selections of words, you can also look for things that taste and smell can *do*. See Figure 3-1.

| SMELL AND TASTE WORDS | |
|---|---|
| **Smell** | **Taste** |
| Other words for *smell*:<br>**Smell as a noun:**<br>    stench, stink, aroma, odor, scent, fragrance, perfume, trace, whiff<br>**Smell as a verb:**<br>    reek, stink | Other words for *taste*:<br>**Taste as a noun:**<br>    flavor, tang<br>**Taste as a verb:**<br>    sample, savor |
| **Verbs—Things that smells can do:**<br>    assault, drift, float, waft, linger, fester, fill, follow, invite, repel, blow, concentrate, hint, hang, spread, envelop, overpower, overwhelm, disgust, hit, surprise | **Verbs—Things that tastes can do:**<br>    fill, overpower, overwhelm, underwhelm, repel, invite, heat-up, disgust, flood, gag, hit, surprise |

This chart is undoubtedly an incomplete list. I always challenge my students to see if they can come up with more. Even with these few words, though, it is possible to create a great many combinations of smell/taste nouns and verbs that will be a great deal livelier than "It smelled bad" or "It tasted good."

This technique can work for the senses of sound and touch as well, if students wish to use it. Sounds can be mentioned as *crashes*, *slams*, and *rattles* that do a variety of things. And sounds can *do* many of the things smells can—they can *drift, fill, repel,* and *hang in the air.* They can also do a lot of things that smells can't. Sounds can *vibrate, echo, reverberate, bounce, fill, murmur, ricochet,* and *reverberate.* And all of them are more interesting than simply saying, "The sound was loud." Sensations like pain, heat, or cold can *travel, flare, stab, move, touch, tickle, tingle, fly, crawl, spread,* or *grow.* The list for sound and touch is nearly endless.

## Sensory Overview

At the beginning of the chapter, I said that when it came to sensory detail, it was more a question of options than rules. The problem is that the options can be overwhelming. To help my students—and myself—keep it all straight, I give them the following review chart to reference as they write.

| WAYS TO USE THE SENSES | | | | | |
|---|---|---|---|---|---|
| Sense → <br> Writing <br> Technique ↓ | Sight | Sound | Touch | Smell | Taste |
| Mention the Sense | I saw the cookie jar falling. | I heard the jar hit the floor with a crash. | A piece of cookie jar hit me on the leg, and it hurt. | The cookies that scattered on the floor still smelled fresh out of the oven. | The cookies tasted sweet. |
| Personal Effects | My eyes grew wide with alarm as I saw the cookie jar falling. | I winced as the jar shattered on the floor. | I flinched as a piece of the jar flew into my leg. | I sniffed at the still-warm cookies now scattered on the floor. | I put a warm cookie in my mouth and licked my lips. |
| Direct Sensory Input | The cookie jar flew into pieces and the cookies spilled out across the floor. | The jar crashed onto the floor. | A shard of the jar pierced my leg. | Not applicable. | Not applicable. |
| "Verb" the Sense | The sight of the cookie jar breaking alarmed me. | The crash echoed down the hall. | The pain in my leg flared up, but then vanished. | The aroma of freshly-baked cookies drifted up from the floor. | The flavor of warm baked cookie and melted chocolate chips filled my mouth. |

# Sensory Writing Exercises

The following exercises are designed to force students to write using all their senses, and to help them have fun doing it. Students will often take these exercises and turn them into full-length essays or stories.

## Sight Unseen Exercises

Many students rely on the sense of sight a lot when they write, to the exclusion of the other senses. I designed these exercises to get rid of the sense of sight, to force students to write only about the other senses. Each scenario is to be a description of the experience of being in that setting, but your details must be limited to sound, smell, and physical sensation. I tell students that nothing much needs to happen in these scenes, but that they must make us experience the setting without using the sense of sight. They nearly always rise to the challenge.

It was pitch black in the forest.

I was so scared, I closed my eyes on the roller coaster.

I fumbled around in the dark after the power went out.

They had blindfolded me, so I couldn't tell where I was.

For this last exercise, number 4, the student writer should decide on a location so that the reader and narrator can figure out where they are. This can be a kidnapping narrative, a "trust" exercise at a camp, or some other situation the student dreams up.

## Sound Exercises

The concert was loud.

The party was noisy.

I listened to the peaceful sounds at the ocean.

As I tried to fall asleep, little noises from outside in my neighborhood kept me awake.

## Touch Exercises

The first two here are deliberately vague. Students can write about whatever place they want that is either hot or cold. They can invent a circumstance, or write from personal experience.

It was too hot.

It was too cold.

I jumped into the water.

I laughed way too hard.

## Smell and Taste Exercises

The meal was fantastic.

The meal was terrible.

The trash can smelled awful.

Fantastic smells wafted from the kitchen window.

# Fiction Sense vs. Nonfiction Sense

The uses of sensory detail in fiction are many and obvious. In fiction, the goal is to immerse the readers in the characters' world—to make them feel as though they are there. But what about nonfiction? A good activity to get students thinking about the role of sensory detail in their essays is to list the senses and ask them what kinds of topics might lend themselves to those particular types of sensory details.

Obviously, taste and smell would come into play with any essay encouraging change in the cafeteria.

Smell might lend itself to an essay on better sanitation. Sound might come in handy in essays about class size—how noisy is a class of 40 as opposed to a class of 20? Touch might come into play in any essay dealing with comfort issues, such as air conditioning on buses. Thinking about topics that might lend themselves to sensory detail helps students think about using it when a real topic comes along.

Movies already come in 3-D with multi-track digital sound, but until they add smell-o-rama or sensory seats, words are still more immersive and interactive than any other medium. Getting students to write using the senses may help them to realize that words are sometimes worth a thousand pictures.

# CHAPTER 4

# Pictures of Places: Atmosphere and Setting

I love to reread books. New books are piled on and around my nightstand, but occasionally I can't resist the urge to reread an old favorite. Obviously, I don't reread books to find out the ending, which I already know. I often reread books to pay a visit to the characters, many of whom feel like old friends. But most often I reread books to revisit a place. Every few years I need to go on a vacation to Narnia, to Middle Earth, to Hogwarts, even to the town of Maycomb, for all its faults.

Of course there are also places I would never want to revisit for real. Tolkien's Mordor and Rowling's Azkaban come to mind. But even horrible settings are horrible because the writing is good. Creating a sense of place is one of the most amazing things any writer can do, but many writers, including me, often struggle with it. Sometimes descriptions are too detailed, but sometimes they're too sketchy.

When I drafted my young adult novel *Making My Escape*, I wrote a first chapter where the protagonist, Daniel Finn, rides all over town on his bicycle doing his paper route. This town is the main setting for the book, yet when one of my friends read the draft, his first comment was, "I couldn't see the town."

The town he rides through was based on my hometown in upstate New York, and I could see it, so I felt no need to describe it to anyone else. The feedback I got, though, caused me to go back into the first chapter and describe the town so my readers could picture it. The problem was, it slowed the chapter down. All of a sudden Daniel, the first-person narrator, was stopping the action to tell us about the narrow streets and Victorian cottages of Bay Lake. It didn't work.

I then hit on an idea. Instead of waiting to introduce the character of Daniel's father in a later chapter, I decided to introduce him in Chapter 1 as the presence of a big blue truck Daniel is trying to avoid. Daniel doesn't want to see his father, but avoiding the big blue truck in Bay Lake is difficult.

> Hiding places, or hanging-out places, were hard to come by in Bay Lake if you couldn't or wouldn't go into a bar. No restaurants, not even a McDonald's. No arcades. No department stores or malls or teen centers. Just little houses. Bay Lake is over a hundred years old, just like some of my paper route customers. Mom has pictures of me as a baby at the Centennial Celebration. They had me dressed up as a cowboy, although I'm not sure why—Bay Lake wasn't settled by cowboys. It was settled by Victorian Methodists who built it as a summer resort for tent revivals. The houses in the middle of the town were originally summer cottages. They look like little gingerbread dollhouses. The front porches are full of ornate Victorian curly-cue patterns carved in wood. Some of the people in town are trying to have us put on the National Register of Historic Places. The only problem is that, outside of the quaint little town center, there isn't another purely "historic" acre in town. Victorian cottages mix with modular homes and trailers in a kind of mishmash.
>
> At any rate, there were only three places to "go" in town: Bill's, the post office, or the library. Since he might stop to pick up mail or beer at the first two places, the obvious choice was the library (pp. 9–10).

I now had a reason to describe the town. It didn't stop the show. Descriptions of places need to have a point—and, as always, avoiding an avalanche of adjectives is paramount.

# Settings From Fiction and Nonfiction

Describing a place is one of the easiest kinds of description to apply to both fiction and nonfiction. Any piece of fiction will have a setting, and many types of nonfiction—e.g., restaurant reviews, references to neighborhoods or schools in newspaper articles, ad copy for vacation spots in travelogues—include descriptions of places. We'll discuss more uses later, but it is easy to find descriptions of places in all kinds of writing.

## Fictional Settings

One of my favorite Looney Toons cartoons is Chuck Jones's "Duck Amuck" starring Daffy Duck (it's available on YouTube and on DVD, and only takes six minutes to show). Daffy begins the movie in front of a background of revolutionary France à la "The Three Musketeers." But as soon as Daffy begins to parry, thrust, and "swashbuckle" (to coin a verb), the background is erased, and suddenly Daffy doesn't know what to do. Then the unseen artist paints a farm. Daffy begins to sing "Daffy Duck he had a farm, e-i-e-i-o . . ." until the farm setting is erased again and is replaced by an arctic setting, whereupon he dons ski gear and begins singing "Jingle Bells." Without a proper, consistent setting, Daffy just doesn't know how to act, or even how to dress. Any fictional character without a proper setting might get just as frustrated as Daffy eventually does.

For a long time, when I would ask my students to analyze fiction, I would have them simply fill in a blank for "the time and place of the story." It seemed that there was nothing else to do, right? But settings can do different things aside from just exist. The narrator in a fictional story shows us the setting so that we have a context for the characters and their actions, but a setting can be more than just a backdrop. The setting may show us things about the character who inhabits it. The setting may be of critical importance to the plot, as in a murder mystery. As usual, I ask students to go back to see what real writers do. How do writers make settings vivid and visible so that their characters are not acting in front of a blank, white nothingness like poor Daffy in Jones's cartoon? And what reasons do they have for describing them?

The following lists are by no means complete, but they do suggest some of the reasons fiction and nonfiction writers describe the settings in their texts.

## Describing for Practical Reasons: Mysteries, Farces, and More

Sometimes descriptions are put into a story for very specific reasons, reasons that don't become clear until the story is over, or nearly so. Many Sherlock Holmes stories contain very specific descriptions of settings because those settings contain both red herrings and important clues as to how the crime was committed. For instance, in "The Adventure of the Speckled Band," Watson describes the furnishings of a room where a mysterious death has occurred, but Holmes himself observes certain details that stand out: a servant's bell-pull that doesn't work, a ventilator between two rooms, and a bed that is bolted to the floor underneath the pull and the ventilator. Those three items are the keys to the solution.

In James Thurber's family farce "The Night the Bed Fell," he even tells us, as the narrator, that "The layout of the rooms and the disposition of their occupants is important to an understanding of what later occurred" (p.5). He then describes the layout of the second floor of the house. "In the front room upstairs (just under father's attic bedroom) were my mother and my brother Terry, who sometimes sang in his sleep, usually 'Marching Through Georgia' or 'Onward, Christian Soldiers.' Briggs Beall and myself were in a room adjoining this one. My brother Roy was in a room across the hall from ours. Our bull terrier, Rex, slept in the hall" (p. 5). All of these details become important to the events that follow, which have people running all over the upper floor, breaking windows, and trying to beat down doors.

Sometimes describing a setting a certain way can have a huge impact on the theme of a book. One of my favorite scenes from a novel is near the end of Harper Lee's *To Kill a Mockingbird*. The narrator, Scout, finally gets to stand on the porch of the mysterious Boo Radley's house, and finds that by standing there, in his shoes, she can see down the street and have a view that encompasses all of the major events of the book. It's important to the plot, and to the theme of "standing in someone else's shoes," that the setting be described that way. A setting can become an embodiment of a story's theme.

When we read a story that uses a setting for practical reasons, I ask students to note how it's described and for what purposes. Many times they glide over the setting, not even thinking.

## Describing to Show Characters' Personalities

If a setting is inhabited by a character, then that setting and what is in it tells us a lot about that character. In "The Sneaker Crisis," by Shirley Jackson, the description of the house and the items that the mother is constantly shifting around tells us a lot about not only the mother but also the rest of the family. Consider Dumbledore's oddly appointed office in the Harry Potter books, the description of the Wonka factory in *Charlie and the Chocolate Factory*, or Mrs. Murray's kitchen lab in *A Wrinkle in Time*. All of those settings tell us something about the characters that inhabit them.

## Describing to Create Context

Most stories are set in some sort of context. A piece of historical fiction needs to establish period details that are believable and show us the social situation the characters are living in. A fantasy or science fiction story usually needs to set up a whole alternate world and introduce us to it through what the characters experience. Even a piece of realistic fiction set in the present day (how rapidly the present becomes a "period piece" these days!) creates context based on where it is set. A story set in a cheery suburb will have a very different kind of context for the characters than a story set in a downtown tenement building. Details help give us context.

## Describing to Create Atmosphere

Atmosphere, the feel of a place, is something I love to see created on the page when I read, and one of the things I try to create when I write. Some stories seem suspenseful from the moment you start reading, simply because of the atmosphere that's created—nothing even has to happen. The atmosphere creates the suspense. But atmosphere can also make things seem magical, cozy, bleak—or dozens of other things. One of the things I find with atmosphere is that students don't have a good working vocabulary for it, so I supply them with a list.

### Fictional Atmospheres—The Many Moods of Settings

sinister (a rainy, dark alley)

magical (an enchanted forest or castle)

gloomy (gray, dreary buildings, dead trees, dark clouds)

humdrum/boring (a suburban neighborhood with cookie-cutter houses)

spooky (haunted houses, dark forests)

festive (a carnival, a circus, a festival)

majestic (mountains reaching into the heavens, or a great cathedral)

gothic (dark, musty cathedral or stone building with statues)

lush (jungles, tropical rain forests, South Seas islands)

oppressive (gloomy, overcrowded apartment buildings or prisons, or even classrooms)

pleasant (small town, country lane)

This list is only partial, to get you thinking!

I remind students that there are plenty of other types of atmosphere, and that these terms can be used to describe settings other than the ones I gave as examples. I ask students to find selections of texts that have atmosphere and to share them, and we look at what helps create those atmospheres. We usually discover a few common threads: climate/weather, buildings and structures, time of day, sensory detail, and lighting. We will touch on lighting again in Chapter 9, which is about cinematic writing techniques, but lighting comes into play here as we look specifically at setting.

## Nonfiction Locations

All of the things that we looked at for fictional settings apply here to nonfiction as well. You can write about a real place for practical reasons, to show us something about a person, or to create context and atmosphere. It simply depends on the purpose of your writing. A persuasive piece might require that we describe a place to call attention to the problems that exist there and give them context. An expository piece about a person might require that we describe a person's workspace or home. A narrative about a historical event might need to give us a practical description that will enable us to understand why things happened the way they did. But nonfiction offers its own specific reasons to describe as well.

### Describing to Flatter or Criticize

If you are writing a review of a restaurant or vacation spot, or writing an advertisement to make a reader want to go to those locations, you will want either to flatter the spot, if you like it or are writing the ad, or criticize it, if you're the critic and are giving it a "thumbs down." How you describe the place creates either a good or bad impression of it.

## Description for Its Own Sake

Unlike fiction, where descriptions usually serve a variety of purposes, sometimes we write nonfiction descriptions just to create descriptions. It can be hard to make it interesting, but if you have real enthusiasm (or non-enthusiasm) for your topic, a pure descriptive piece can be fun and interesting to read. Even with a straight description for its own sake, though, there is usually a *point*, an attitude about the place the author wants to convey.

That idea of having a point is key. It doesn't have to be a profound point, but there needs to be a point nonetheless, and we seldom ask students to think about that point when we ask them to describe. As we read descriptions of places in essays, short fiction, and novels, and share them from the novels they are reading, we need to look not only at *how* the author describes a place, but also at *why*.

# An Introduction to Describing a Place: The Messy Room

This is a clichéd topic, I know. I've seen it in various places as a topic for a long time, but I've seldom seen much explanation of how to get students to turn the topic into a really good paragraph. My early attempts at it yielded sentences like, "There was stuff everywhere," "It was really a dump," "It was scummy," and "It was really, really messy." No pictures there.

But I like this particular topic because it is somehow innately appealing to the middle-school mind—few can resist the allure of making a big, fat mess, even if it is only on paper. Students almost want to compete with each other to make their mess messier than their neighbor's. It is also a topic anyone can write about—we've all seen messy rooms, somewhere. If nowhere else, my students have at least seen my classroom at its worst (which is far too often, sadly). The main reason I like this topic, though, is that it also lends itself to teaching the kind of specificity that I want them to use when they write. So before they write, we discuss what they are going to write.

## Concrete Nouns

I ask the class about this sentence I got from a student during my first year of teaching: "There was stuff everywhere."

"Can you see that?" I ask.

Some students say they can see the "stuff" that is "everywhere," but when pressed, they have to admit that the "stuff" could be anything, and it could be anywhere in the room. Saying there is stuff everywhere is scarcely better than saying the room is messy.

I then ask them to give me a piece of specific "stuff." Sometimes a sharp student will nail it right away and say something like "a sweat sock," but usually they'll give me a category, like "toys" or "clothes." I actually relish it when they do, because then we can get more specific, step by step.

"What kind of toy?" I ask.

"A board game," someone answers.

"Which board game?"

"Clue."

"Is it open or closed?"

"Open."

"What's spilling out of it?"

"Characters and weapons."

"Which characters? Which weapons?"

"Col. Mustard, Mrs. Peacock, a wrench, and a candlestick."

"Now we're on to something."

Or the discussion might go from clothes to underwear, to white Fruit of the Loom briefs. In any case, we talk about the fact that the more specific the details are, the better.

Then we talk about the "everywhere" part of the "stuff everywhere" equation. Where are these specific items? We begin to list places for the items to hang out: on the wall, the ceiling fan, the bed, the desk, the floor, the dresser, the window sill; under the bed, the pillow, the desk, or the dresser; in the closet, the drawers, or the desk. There are all kinds of places for things to be.

Now comes the hard part. What will those things *do* in all those places?

## Inanimate Strong Verbs

As I discussed in Chapter 1, I tell my students to use "dead verbs" sparingly. Some are okay, but too many in a paragraph starts to slow it down. "There were clothes on the floor. There was a pizza under the bed." The problem with description is that the details in a place, especially indoors, tend to just, well, sit there. They are, after all, *inanimate* objects, unless we're writing *Toy Story* and they come to life when we're not looking. How do students use strong verbs with inanimate objects? It might seem like a contradiction in terms, but even things that are just lying around can come to life with the right verbs.

---

There are plenty of strong verbs to describe the "action" of still objects, even if some of them have *were* or *was* attached to them. I usually start with one or two examples, write them on the board, and ask for volunteers to help me add to the list, which often ends up looking something like this: *hung, stuck, piled, spilled, draped, tumbled, jammed, sat, crammed, overflowed, towered, hid, peeked out, climbed, teetered, barricaded, scattered, blended, plopped, plunked, billowed, swayed . . .*

The list could go on, but a list as long as that is usually more than enough. By the time you have brainstormed enough concrete nouns and specific verbs, the problem won't be coming up with details, but limiting yourself to the details you like the best. And if students layer in some sensory smells as well, the messy room will be as jam-packed with pictures as it is with "stuff."

## Avoiding "Over the Top" Details

One caution: beware students who go "over the top" in their details. The room is messy, not disgusting beyond all possible hope of redemption! We'll get to hyperbole later, and there is room for overblown statements such as "When you walked in the room, you needed snow shoes to get over the piles of clothes." But some students simply decide to go all out in the gross department and write things like this: "There was an eight-foot pile of cow manure in the corner!" or "There were 8,000 rats in the room!" I try to encourage them to go for small-scale disgusting; it's far better to tell us about the greasy paper plate sitting under the bed with a half- eaten piece of moldy pizza with a cockroach scuttling across it.

This exercise gives the students some basic tools to work with when they write descriptions of things other than a messy room. The more specific their nouns and strong verbs are, the better.

# Group Exercise: Generic House

Another activity I use to get writers thinking about how details change our perception of a setting involves giving groups of students a "generic" passage to revise. The trick is that each group revises its paragraph to make the house a more specific kind of place by adding details between the lines.

After the groups have added their details, I ask students to share their revised paragraphs. The other groups have to guess what type of house it is, or what type of person lives there, and we discuss how the word choices helped make it clear what type of house it was.

# Writing Exercises
• • • • • • • • • • • • • • • • • • • • • • • •

The following exercises give students a chance to try out their descriptive skills on very specific topics. Of course, I try to follow these exercises with an assignment that allows them to choose their own topic—a description of a favorite place, for instance. As students begin working on these exercises and assignments, I remind them that they have several techniques at their disposal when it comes to describing a place, including the following:

- Use concrete nouns
- Use strong verbs, even for inanimate objects
- Use weather and time of day to create atmosphere
- Use sensory detail
- Have a focus: create a sense of time, a sense of place, a sense of character, or a sense of atmosphere

With these tools in mind, I ask my students to create word pictures about some of the following places. Note that nearly all of these topics imply atmosphere of some kind.

- The car was a piece of junk. (I know a car may not seem like a place, but if it's not a place, what exactly is it? It's too big and detailed to be a mere object. I maintain that it is, indeed, a place.)
- I looked at my dream car in the parking lot.
- The classroom was interesting.
- The classroom was dull. (The room is dull, not the teacher or the class.)
- The house was spooky-looking.

4-1

Generic House

Take the paragraph about a house below and revise it. Make it more specifically a _____ house.

The house was big. The front lawn had plants and trees. The front door was large. The rooms were large and filled with furniture. The windows were big, too. Pictures hung on the walls. Potted plants were in every room. The banquet table in the dining room was piled high with food. A large staircase led to a balcony on the second story, which had numerous bedrooms, each with its own balcony looking out over the gardens. The gardens had many more plants. The library had lots of books. The kitchen had many cabinets and appliances and lots of dishes, utensils, and cooking implements. The walls were tall and the ceilings were high. It was a big house.

Make it more specifically a _____ house.
farmer's
millionaire's
haunted
abandoned
recently burglarized
tacky, shoddy, and vulgar
neat freak's
rock star's
movie star's
criminal's

Teaching Students to Make Writing Visual & Vivid

- The restaurant made you want to stay for hours.
- The restaurant was a "dive."
- The city street had a sinister feel.
- The forest was beautiful.
- The forest seemed to close in around me.
- The carnival was full of sound and light.
- The mountains towered above me.
- The old stone mansion looked grim.
- The jungle was hot and full of life.
- The hallway at school was overcrowded.
- The small town street was quiet in the evening.

Pick and choose the exercises that might appeal to your students or help them best develop their descriptive "muscles." Of course, these are merely exercises. The proof comes when you set them lose on their own topics—descriptive essays, restaurant reviews, travelogues, narratives, or expository essays that require them to create a sense of place.

# CHAPTER 5

# Pictures of People: Appearances in Context

It might seem simple to describe a person's appearance. Write down a bunch of details about how he or she looks—facial features, hair, clothing, shoes—and the job is done, right? But it is not as simple as it looks. When my students write fiction, I ask them to think about what their characters *look* like before they begin. What color hair and eyes do they have? How do they dress? What body type are they? What shade is their skin? After listing these details on a prewriting worksheet, my students sometimes go to their stories and introduce their characters with sentences that sound something like this:

> Darla was five feet three inches tall. She had brownish-blond hair, and her eyes were brown, too. She wore jeans and T-shirts. She wore Nike sneakers. She was pale and skinny and weighed about a hundred and twenty-five pounds. Her friend Brad was five feet eight inches tall, which meant he was five inches taller than Darla. He had black hair and blue eyes. He wore loose-fitting jeans and white tank tops. He had a deep tan from being at the beach all the time. He wore a baseball cap, and he weighed about one hundred and forty-five pounds.

Of course, I have no one but myself to blame. The students who wrote passages like the one above were giving me exactly what I asked for—a list of details. But details themselves aren't enough. A description needs to have context—it needs to have a *point*, and a point is sorely lacking in descriptions like this one of Darla and Brad. Sometimes presentation is the important thing, and that's why writing descriptions of people isn't as easy as it looks.

Describing every last detail of how a person looks is not only impractical in most instances; it also becomes monotonous to read, as we saw in the example above. And description is difficult, as we saw in the last chapter, because it doesn't lend itself to strong, lively verbs. People wear clothes, but what do the clothes do? What does hair do? What do glasses do? We tend to end up simply saying, "He wore . . ." over and over again. So how do we fix these problems? In this chapter we'll attempt to answer some of those questions, and we'll do it, as always, by looking at what real writers do.

## Principles From Published Writers

Writers tend to describe people for particular reasons, in service to something else in the piece. In character-driven fiction, everything in the story will be there to reveal character, just as in a biography or profile, every detail is there to tell us something about the real person. A murder mystery or piece of historical fiction may pay a lot of attention to the specific details of a character's appearance, either to plant clues or to create period authenticity. But in a plot-heavy story or an event-heavy account, people's looks or personalities are only important to the extent that they influence the events in the story. Getting students to think about issues like these makes them not only write better, but also read more attentively as they look at what authors focus on in their descriptions.

Although we tend to ask students to go into a lot of detail about characters, describing people is often a case where less is more. In older classic novels, we often find that the story will stop for longer, more detailed descriptions of characters. Modern fiction, on the other hand, tends toward picking a few details to create a vivid sketch of a character. Find any recent novel and look through the first few pages of exposition to find the introductory descriptions of the characters. They usually pack a ton of information into a very tight space, as these examples demonstrate:

From *The True Confessions of Charlotte Doyle* by Avi:

"Mr. Grummage was dressed in a black frock coat with a stove pipe hat that added to his considerable height. His somber, sallow face registered no emotion. His eyes might have been those of a dead fish" (p. 7).

In this brief description, we find out this is a period piece, probably set in the 1800s, and we learn a lot about the personality of the character.

From *A Ring of Endless Light* by Madeleine L'Engle:

"He was tall and thinnish—not skinny—and his hair was what Rob calls hair-colored hair, not quite brown, not quite blond, like mine. His eyes were open, and there was somehow light behind them, the way sometimes the light on the ocean seems to come from beneath the water, rather than just being reflected from above. He was standing in a relaxed manner, but a little muscle in his cheek was twitching just slightly, so he wasn't as easy as he seemed" (p. 9).

Here we get physical details, and a sense that the narrator is observing a complex, rounded character.

From "The Rule of Names" by Ursula K. LeGuin, a short story from *The Wind's Twelve Quarters:*
"Mr. Underhill came out from under his hill, smiling and breathing hard. Each breath shot out of his nostrils as a double puff of steam, snow-white in the morning sunshine. Mr. Underhill looked up at the bright December sky and smiled wider than ever, showing snow-white teeth" (p. 101).

This description, from the very first lines of the story, not only conveys that Mr. Underhill is a little creepy—it also tells us something about the magical setting of the story, and foreshadows that there might be something mysterious about Mr. Underhill.

In *Number the Stars,* by Lois Lowry, the descriptions of main characters are very brief, and they are written in a way that contrasts the two characters' looks: "She [Ellen] was a stocky ten-year-old, unlike lanky Annemarie" (p. 1). "Annemarie's silvery bond hair flew behind her, and Ellen's dark pigtails bounced against her shoulders" (p. 1).

In a novel I recently wrote with my eighth-grade son Christopher, we introduced the main character, Ian Portent, in the very first paragraph:

"I wonder where my socks went again," Ian Portent asked himself, peering into his family's clothes dryer. He had pulled out all his socks, and, once again, half of them were missing—the half that left him with nine single, mismatched socks, to be precise. It made him crazy. People at school had started making fun of him because of his socks, calling him 'hobo boy' and 'Captain Clueless,' though if it hadn't been the socks, they would have found other things to taunt him about, and usually did. If it wasn't his smarts or ghostly paleness, it was his small stature and thin frame, or maybe that he was two years younger than the rest of the eighth-grade class. But it was usually the socks" (p. 9).

Our goal here was to set up a basic premise of the book—that things keep vanishing around their house—and use that idea to reveal something about Ian's appearance and how that appearance affects his social life. The point is, a description needs a point.

I make this point about points to my students by having them read the passages above, or others like them, and try to figure out what the point is. (Notice the sneaky way I'm slipping in a reading skill here.) See Figure 5.1 for a worksheet version.

So we know that writers have a lot of potential details to work with, but they usually

5-1: This worksheet activity can be used to get students thinking about how character descriptions focus on specific character traits.

The authors of the character descriptions below do not describe their characters head to toe. Instead, they choose details with a particular focus in mind. Underneath each description, write down the focus, or focuses of each description:

From *The True Confessions of Charlotte Doyle* by Avi: "Mr. Grummage was dressed in a black frock coat with a stove pipe hat that added to his considerable height. His somber, sallow face registered no emotion. His eyes might have been those of a dead fish." (7)

This description focuses on:

From *A Ring of Endless Light* by Madeleine L'Engle: "He was tall and thinnish—not skinny—and his hair was what Rob calls hair-colored hair, not quite brown, not quite blond, like mine. His eyes were open, and there was somehow light behind them, the way sometimes the light on the ocean seems to come from beneath the water, rather than just being reflected from above. He was standing in a relaxed manner, but a little muscle in his cheek was twitching just slightly, so he wasn't as easy as he seemed." (9)

This description focuses on:

From "The Rule of Names" by Ursula K. LeGuin from *The Wind's Twelve Quarters:* "Mr. Underhill came out from under his hill, smiling and breathing hard. Each breath shot out of his nostrils as a double puff of steam, snow-white in the morning sunshine. Mr. Underhill looked up at the bright December sky and smiled wider than ever, showing snow-white teeth." (101)

This description focuses on:

From *Number the Stars,* by Lois Lowry: "She [Ellen] was a stocky ten-year-old, unlike lanky Annemarie." "Annemarie's silvery bond hair flew behind her, and Ellen's dark pigtails bounced against her shoulders." (1)

This description focuses on:

From *Portents* by David and Christopher Finkle: "I wonder where my socks went again," Ian Portent asked himself, peering into his family's clothes dryer. He had pulled out all his socks, and, once again, half of them were missing—the half that left him with nine single, mismatched socks, to be precise. It made him crazy. People at school had started making fun of him because of his socks, calling him "hobo boy" and "Captain Clueless," though if it hadn't been the socks, they would have found other things to taunt him about, and usually did. If it wasn't his smarts or ghostly paleness, it was his small stature and thin frame, or maybe that he was two years younger than the rest of the eighth-grade class. But it was usually the socks. (1)

This description focuses on:

tend to focus on a few key details to help them make the specific points they want to make. How can we get students to do the same? The following writing exercise helps students do just that.

# The Suspects

• • • • • • • • • • • • • • • • • • • • • • • • • • • • • • • • • • • • • • • • • • • • • • • • • • • • • • • • •

The following assignment is one I have tweaked over the years. At first it was a simple exercise in "more detail is better detail." But as I kept using this assignment in class, I added to it, and it became an exercise not just in *using* details, but in *choosing* details.

The first thing you need is two fairly large pictures of two different people. I drew my two suspects on sheets of craft paper from our Media Center ten years ago, and I've been using them ever since. I have included two black-and-white line drawings of them in the Appendix, page 149. If you want to use the drawings, feel free to copy them onto transparencies and then use the overhead to trace them onto paper. They're a little odd-looking (see below), but they work. You can find photographs online or in magazines, take original photographs to your specifications, draw your own as I did, or get someone—a student or faculty member—to draw for you. If you could copy a couple of photographs onto transparencies and borrow a second overhead projector, that works, too.

## Day One

In any case, here's the basic set-up. I divide my room in half, equal seating on both sides, facing the middle. I then put something in the middle of the classroom, some kind of divider that can have a picture on each side of it, one for each half of the class to see. I've used a magazine rack on a table, an art easel, some stacked desks— whatever works. I am currently fortunate enough to have an

5-2 and 5.3: Photographs of the large drawings I display in class for the "suspect" activity

actual folding screen that works beautifully. The photos at right show how it works in my classroom.

Have students take out a sheet of paper and label it "My Suspect," and then give them their imaginary scenario. "You are on field trip to a museum. This museum has a ton of valuable artifacts, but the most valuable, worth millions of dollars, is the huge, fantastic Baseball Diamond!" (Ba-dum-dum. Wait for the groan.) "You were each given little notebooks to take notes about what interested you. As you are leaving the museum, this half of the room is with one chaperone group, and this half with another chaperone group at the other end of the lobby." (Add teacher names for their chaperones here to spice things up.) "As you are waiting for the bus, each group sees a shady, suspicious-looking character leaving the museum, walking slowly, trying to seem casual. The alarm begins to sound. You are going to take some quick notes on the person before he or she vanishes. I'm going to show you your suspect now . . ."

5-4: Students on one side of the class describe their suspect but are unable to see the other group's suspect.

5-5: Students on the opposite side of the room do the same, describing only the suspect they can see.

At this point I reveal the two pictures, each one visible to only half the room. I give students exactly two minutes to jot down a list of as many details as they can remember. I tell them the police will want this information, because the Baseball Diamond has been stolen. When the two minutes are up, I hide the drawings again. I tell them that the police want them to write up descriptions of the suspects for their police artists—and to not leave out any detail. The students' task is then to write a one-paragraph description of the suspect. (Give them a time limit, from 10 to 20 minutes.) Before they start writing, we discuss the fact that they should avoid writing in fragments. The guidelines I write on the board look something like this:

*Write in complete sentences:*

*Wrong (fragment): Blue eyes, purple hair, missing teeth.*

*Better, but dull (complete sentence): He had blue eyes, purple hair, and missing teeth.*

*Best (complete sentences, strong verbs): His blue eyes contrasted with his shocking purple hair. Jagged teeth nearly filled his mouth, except for the black gaping holes where they were missing.*

Here is a sample "witness" paragraph from April, one of my sixth graders:

> A pale old woman with a suspicious look walked in. She had pink, slicked back hair, pale green eyes, and a big black mole under her left eye. She had a remarkably good cheekbone structure, but exaggerated makeup. I quickly noticed her shimmering gold hoop earring and pearl necklace. She clutched the handle of a green and pink umbrella in her right hand, and a pink purse in her left, which almost matched her long, painted fingernails. She wore a purple floral dress and a lavender trench coat. There's something not right about this woman.

As students are writing, I pass out a single sheet of white copy paper to each of them. At this juncture, some of them guess what we're up to. When the writing time is nearly up, I give them a couple of warnings, and then call time. I have one student collect all the papers for side A, and another for side B. I then say, "You are about to change roles. You are no longer witnesses. You are police artists. You will be receiving a description of a suspect you have never seen. Your job is to produce a drawing that contains every detail mentioned in the paragraph. If you don't think you draw that well, that's okay. The only thing that matters is somehow including every detail from the paragraph you receive. At the top of your white paper, write 'Police Artist:' followed by your name. Under that write 'Witness:' followed by the person who wrote the paragraph you're about to get."

My two helpers then redistribute the paragraphs at random to the opposite side of the room. I give students about ten minutes to quickly draw their police artist renderings. This usually becomes quite a humorous activity. Students will complain about each other's penmanship, clarity, and spelling. That's okay. They are finding out how important these things are. I'll let them write a polite, "Please work on your _____" at the bottom of the page if the flaws in the paragraph were distracting. When the time limit is nearly up, I start circulating staplers, and students staple the essays over

5-6: Drawing of the female suspect, created by a student using only a classmate's description

5-7: Drawing of the male suspect from the other side or the room

their drawings. Once time is called and all the essays/drawings are stapled together, I let the students from one side return the essay to its author, then vice versa.

When students see what their paragraphs turned into when someone else drew them, it's usually quite funny—but also powerful. After the chatter has died down, I remind them of what Stephen King says, that "writing is mental telepathy."

I tell them, "You have just used words to essentially 'beam' a picture across the room and into someone's head. And they just sent it back to you as a picture. That's what words can do. It's magic!"

By then, a 45-minute class is very close to being over, so I collect the papers. This lesson never fails to be listed as a favorite of students at the end of the year, and as one that they learned the most from. But that's just the first day. What comes next is just as interesting.

## Day Two

I grade students' initial paragraphs on their level of detail and on how well they described their suspect using some sentence variety rather than listing or using fragments. When we meet again, I introduce them to the concept that when authors describe people, they do so with particular focuses in mind. I project fictional descriptions like the ones near the start of this chapter in Figure 5-1, and we discuss the focus of each one. Authors may want to tell us something about the time period, the character's personality, or the character's emotions (more on those in the next chapter). Or the author may simply want to contrast the looks between two characters in a striking way so we can keep them straight in our heads as we read, as in Lois Lowry's *Number the Stars*. Once I have made students aware of how authors use brief, narrow descriptions to focus on what really matters for that character, I hand back their original paragraphs, post the drawings of the suspects again, and ask them to take out a new paper. This is "The Suspects—Part 2."

They now write four shorter, two-to-four sentence descriptions, but each one is focused on a specific narrative purpose. For each of these topics, they write for three or four minutes, then share them with each other to see if they used similar details. We share some aloud with the whole class, then move on to the next one.

> He/she has lots of places to hide a stolen object. (I start with this one because it's the easiest to write about—the students actually look at both people for hiding places.)
>
> He/she just came from _____. (Students have to invent somewhere he or she might have just arrived from, then use details from the picture to support that idea.)
>
> He/she is suspicious-looking. (This topic is more abstract, but there are still obvious, specific things to focus on.)
>
> He/she is a good/bad dresser. (This is a matter of opinion, of course. But it will also demonstrate to the students that their attitude toward their subject determines their focus and tone.)

I know this is a lot of explanation for one activity, but I have found it to be an incredibly valuable one. It teaches students some important principles:

- When you describe a person, you send a picture into your reader's head.
- Details matter when describing a person.
- The purpose of your description determines which details you focus on.

Here are a couple of samples of April's short "focus" descriptions:

> **She had lots of places to hide a stolen object.** Her magenta handbag bulged with stuff. Was the diamond in there? Or maybe her long, painted nails on her bony hand had slipped it into her trench coat pocket, or even, possibly, her large, closed umbrella. Why else was she holding it so cautiously?

**She is suspicious-looking.** Her pale eyes looked in a certain direction, trying to signal her eyes elsewhere. Her slick, grim smile stretched across her face. What was she up to? Maybe she was trying to hide something.

Once these basic principles involved in good descriptions have been established, it is easy to transfer them to other writing situations.

# Writing Exercises

The following exercises are designed to get students playing around with details and the focus of those details. They are isolated to keep students focused on the surface. The next chapter will involve combining looks with actions.

## Menu Descriptions

Before starting this activity, I ask students to choose two random digits, one through five. I then reveal two menus, one of adjectives, one of types of characters or people. Their task is to physically describe this person, no matter how oxymoronic he or she may seem. You can make up your own list, but the one I usually use looks like this:

| Adjective | Type of Person |
|---|---|
| 1. Nerdy | 1. Surfer |
| 2. Fashion-obsessed | 2. Rock musician |
| 3. Slobby | 3. Science whiz |
| 4. Neat | 4. "Bookworm" |
| 5. "Goth" or punk | 5. Athlete |

Working out what a nerdy surfer or a fashion-obsessed bookworm would look like presents a certain amount of challenge, but also a certain amount of stereotype-breaking fun.

## Homework—People Watching

This is the real-world equivalent of "The Suspects" assignment, only we hope there are no real criminals involved. I tell students to look out their front windows, get a parent to take them to a park, or merely look out the window as they are riding in the car. Spot interesting people, try to take in as much detail as you can about one of them, and then write descriptions that try to capture them. Again—every detail isn't necessary. Picking the details that give us a quick impression of the person is what's most important. I tell students to be subtle about their people watching—they shouldn't be mistaken for stalkers.

Another variation, if observing real people proves too difficult, is to write descriptions of people in newspaper or magazine photographs. What details stand out? What captures the essence of the person?

# Writing About People in Context

As students write original fiction or essays, I remind them to keep our principles in mind—use specific details about how person looks, but focus on the details that pertain to the situation. Have a *point*. In fiction we focus on physical details for a very practical reason: to help readers keep characters straight in their heads, but also to show readers things about characters' personalities, settings, jobs, and social status.

Describing how people look may seem like more of a fictional technique, but many times essay writers use description for a variety of purposes. There are obvious uses for describing people in some of the old standby writing prompts: school uniforms, groups at school, or the description of a hero. But there are other, more sophisticated, nonfiction reasons for describing how a person looks. When you are asking students to brainstorm support for their own unprompted writing, ask them to consider where a description of a person might come in handy to make a point. Describing a person who is suffering from a particular problem may highlight and create sympathy for that problem.

For almost any topic imaginable, using an example of a specific person puts a face on your topic, makes it less abstract. When my student J. D. wrote his "This I Believe" essay this year, he talked about serving dinner at an interfaith homeless kitchen. He wrote,

> One person there stuck out to me. There was a little girl who came in with her mom and her sister, and her mother looked to be sick. With a smile on her face she walked over to me and put up her dirty hands for me to give her some bread. Before we started the three-hour shift, I was told to only give one dinner roll per person, but when I handed her a first roll, I couldn't help but give her one more. When she went back to her family, she still had that smile on her face.

Not a huge amount of detail here, but a huge impact in the essay. He gave his belief a face.

Sometimes you might describe how a person looks to create one impression, only to create a different one by showing us how the person acts in contrast to their looks the very next moment—which brings us to our next chapter: creating pictures of how people *act*.

# CHAPTER 6

# Pictures of Personalities: Actions and Emotions

**N**oting physical appearances is really less than half the picture when it comes to describing people. Once we've noticed how people look, we start to notice other things—how they act, what emotions they seem to be feeling, and what they say. Whether the people our students are writing about are fictional or real, it is one thing to tell us they are bossy or sweet, happy or sad, outgoing or shy—it is something else entirely to *show* us.

Part of the challenge may be that students are often unaware of body and facial language—their own or anybody else's.

# Pictures of Personalities—How People Act

I will sometimes ask classes to think about a book character that they either liked or hated. I then ask them to think about what those characters *did* that made you like or hate them. In the case of J. K. Rowling's still popular *Harry Potter* books, many students say they like Professor Dumbledore because he listens to Harry, has a good sense of humor, yet is also wise, and calm in the face of danger. I'll then ask them to list specific scenes where Dumbledore listens or shows his sense of humor, his wisdom, or his calm. They usually can. On the other hand, many readers of the saga absolutely hate Dolores Umbridge from the fifth book. Stephen King called her one of the worst villains in modern literature. Asked to list the things she does that made them hate her, students can list all kinds of actions: enacting horrible school rules, making Harry write with a quill that etches bloody cuts into the back of his hand, and banning him from Quidditch for life.

I use examples from Rowling's series because they are so widely known, but any text that describes a person or character's personality will do to make the point. And the point is that authors make us feel things about characters, not by telling us what they are like using adjectives, but by telling us what they *do*, using verbs.

## Indirect Characterization—Samples From Writers

I still teach my students the old-fashioned literature terms, and that includes the pair of terms *direct characterization* and *indirect characterization*. Direct characterization is, of course, when you basically tell us which dwarf your character is: Dopey, Sleepy, Sneezy, and so on. You can even add some adjectives beyond the original Disney seven. Indirect characterization involves *showing* us characters' personalities through their actions. And actions have a language all their own.

As teachers and lifelong readers, we're aware that characters' personalities are developed through their actions, but students may need this pointed out to them. As we read short fiction in class, I try to identify character actions that reveal character personality. For example, in John Bell Clayton's "The White Circle," we read that a character named Anvil, after knocking the narrator down and pinning him to the rocky ground, "ran a finger back into his jaw to dislodge a fragment of apple from his teeth. For a moment he examined the fragment and then wiped it on my cheek." This one disgusting action tells us that Anvil is not just a bully, but a *hateful* bully. In "The Night the Bed Fell," by James Thurber, he doesn't just tell us his relatives were eccentric, he shows us. He writes that his Aunt Gracie Shoaf "was confident that burglars had been getting into her house every night for forty years. The fact that she never missed anything was to her no proof to the contrary. She always claimed that she scared them off before they could take anything, by throwing shoes down the hallway." Actions may be louder than words, but when we write, words are how we show people's actions.

## Drama Games

I've occasionally had the privilege of directing teen theater plays and camps, and they offer a great opportunity to show students that actions sometimes do speak louder than words. When you play a character on stage, I tell them, you must show the audience who that character is before you ever open your mouth. You show them who the character is by how you act and how you walk. The next two exercises are ones we play to help students understand what it takes to establish characters on stage. They are also great for helping students understand how to establish characters on the written page. For both of the following games, I ask half the class to remain seated with writing paper ready. The other half of the class stands and moves to one end of the room. They are the actors. As the actors act, the writers write down what they are seeing. If your classroom is too crowded, you may want to take them outside, weather permitting, or use only a few students at a time as actors. Also, some students may not feel comfortable in the role of actor, so I give those students permission to sit out.

## Walk the Walk

This game is very simple. You tell the actors to walk to the other side of the room, either across the front or from front to back, so the writers can observe what they are doing. The catch is, the actors have to walk like certain kinds of characters. I hold up a sign that only the actors can see to tell them their roles. Here is a list of some of the characters they might walk as:

- A fussy librarian
- A star football player walking onto the field
- A person walking through a dark, spooky forest
- A bodybuilder showing off at the beach
- A person who is running late for an important meeting (no literal running)
- A very senior citizen
- A soldier
- A politician who's campaigning
- A shoplifter
- A rock star making an entrance

As the actors walk, the writers should take some very quick notes about what the actors are doing, and then guess what role they are playing. It is a bit like a game of charades, but also has a point. The students are seeing how simply showing us how a character walks gives us a lot of information about that character.

I usually switch the actors and the writers around about halfway through the exercise. When everyone has had a chance to both write and act, I ask students to pick one of their "character notes" and write a short description of what this character was doing, including their guess as to what it was. We then pair-share these descriptions, and have volunteers share them with the class. I'll ask for description number one first, and so on, and reveal the roles that were on the signs. The actors get to find out how good a job they are doing; the writers get to find out if they were right. But even if a writer is wrong and says a politician was a movie star, she still has a description that fits her wrong guess.

## Flash-Fiction Exercises—Show Us a Personality

The following exercises involve taking behavior beyond the way a character walks to show us how they act and how they interact with others. These topics are fairly relevant to most middle school students, so I caution them not to write about a single real person they may know, but rather to compile behaviors from several real snobs or instigators into one composite character.

- He/she was a total snob.
- He/she was a great student.
- He/she was not the best student.
- He/she was an instigator.
- He/she was a peacemaker.

These exercises sometimes lead to interesting discussions. In particular, the "great student," and "not the best student" descriptions lead to a discussion of how details can be framed in particular ways. The poor student is usually described in negative terms by everyone. Interestingly, though, the great student is often described in negative terms by half the class, too. They view the good student as a "kiss-up" and a "teacher's pet."

Looking at two descriptions of a great student—one positive, one negative—gives us a chance to see how the same personality type can be viewed as good or bad, depending on the point of view of the narrator or speaker. This is important to remember. A description in the first person may be very different, depending on who's doing the describing. We discuss why (for the purposes of this exercise) we will be negative toward both good students *and* low-performing students. Are people jealous of good students? Is the school culture hostile toward good students? We also note that most students know exactly which behaviors lead to either good grades or bad grades (everyone in the room who wrote described those behaviors, after all), yet many students still choose to engage in the behaviors that lead to bad grades. Similar discussions can come out of the peacemaker/instigator exercises. This kind of discussion is good to remind our students, and ourselves, that one of the reasons we write is to discover things about ourselves and the world around us.

# Pictures of Emotions

In Chapter 2 I discussed the "angry teacher" scenario I act out for the class. When I bring up the idea of showing emotions, I remind them of this scenario. I point out that it was at heart a display of emotion, and that emotions must be demonstrated, not just labeled.

## Drama Game—Levels of Emotion

I am uncertain where the following game came from—it came to me through theater circles. It's similar to "Walk the Walk" from above but a bit more complicated. Ask for volunteers who are not terribly self-conscious to be the actors this time. The setup is the same—actors and writers—but this time the actors don't necessarily have to walk in a straight line across the room. They can also simply stand, or they can mill around aimlessly. I give the students emotions to act out—but there's a catch. I, the teacher, can change the level of intensity for the emotions, one being the lowest intensity and ten being the highest. So if I say "Sad, level one," students will start out at a very low level of emotion, simply looking sad, perhaps. By the time you take them to level five, they are probably crying, but not too loudly. Take them to a ten and students will be wailing and carrying on quite dramatically.

A couple of cautions. Students must not make any physical contact with each other, especially if they are acting out *angry*. They can stomp and throw their hands up in the air, but not actually hit anything or anyone. Emotions that are good to act out include *sad, happy, angry, frustrated, amazed, scared, disgusted,* and *disappointed*. Of course, while the actors act, the other students are making notes about what the actors are doing. How do these emotions appear when people act them out? Instead of guessing what the emotions are, I have them make a couple of notes about what the emotions look like at each level.

We save these notes for the writing exercises we'll be doing later.

## Drawing Exercise—Emoticons

Facial expressions, even more than body language, can tell us what a person is feeling. Writing about smiling or frowning can be easy. "He smiled." "She frowned." Or is it easy? A smile can be sincere or insincere, jubilant or resigned, even good or evil. And there are many other types of facial expressions, each with its own individual variations.

In *Making Comics*, cartoonist Scott McCloud claims that there are six basic emotional facial expressions, which are like primary colors: anger, disgust, fear, joy, sadness, surprise (p. 83). Each of the six expressions can have different degrees of emotion (like the drama game above). Anger, for instance, can range from sternness to indignation to rage. All other emotions are mixtures of different levels of these six basic expressions. For instance, anger + disgust = outrage,

6-1: These "smiley face" drawings of the six basic human emotions are fairly easy for almost anyone to draw.

and fear + joy = desperation. Our point with student writers is to get them thinking about how faces relate these different emotions, and how to translate those facial expressions into words.

Most students like to draw, even if they feel they aren't good at it. This exercise is very simple—it's a variation on the "smiley face" or the "frowny face." I ask students to draw a series of circles on their papers, or give them a worksheet with ready-made circles. I then give them the six primary emotions and ask them to draw those emotions as smiley faces. They have only three lines (a mouth and two eyebrows) and two dots (the eyes) to work with. But it's amazing how those few lines can be manipulated to show a huge variety of emotions.

Once we've drawn the basic emotions, I let them try a few more-complex ones: confusion, betrayal, horror, grief. I then ask them to pick one or two and write a sentence to describe the face they've drawn. We discuss how writers can show emotions by describing facial expressions.

## First-Person Feelings—Sensory Emotion

What if you are writing about your own emotions, or the emotions of a first-person narrator? Unless you want your speaker or narrator looking in the mirror constantly, you can't show facial expressions, because you are inside your own face, so to speak. You can describe your own body language, and sometimes refer to what your face is doing, but as the person narrating the emotion from the inside, you have access to one other thing: sensation.

A limited palate of sensations is involved in most of the emotions, but there are endless variations on how to present them. One way to get students thinking about what emotions feel like, physically, is to have them write down the symptoms of different emotions. For example:

| Emotion | Physical Symptom |
| --- | --- |
| Anger | heart pounding, temple throbbing, fists clenched, mouth tightening |
| Disgust | churning stomach, shuddering, curling lip, flaring nostrils, lump moving up and down throat, eyes squinting |
| Fear | heart pounding, hands shaking, blood pounding in temples, catching breath, goose bumps, palms sweating |
| Joy | butterflies in stomach, feeling weightless |
| Sadness | tightening of chest, tears welling up |
| Surprise | jolt through nerves, eyes widening, jumping back |

The lists will vary, but these are all ways of "showing" what an emotion does to your body. Some of them are actions as well, but they are actions that relate to the body's reaction to experiences. I then ask students to put all three elements of emotion—body language, facial expression, and sensation—together in a series of flash-fiction exercises.

## Flash Fiction—Shows of Emotion

As students begin writing these exercises, I tell them that the challenge is to not mention the emotion or any of its synonyms in the paragraph proper. I ask students to include facial expressions, body language, and sensory detail in their descriptions. Someone reading the paragraph without benefit of the topic sentence should still be able to recognize the emotion.

Here are some of the prompts I use in flash-fiction exercises:

- I/he/she was nervous as I/he/she brought home the worst report card ever.
- I/he/she was happy as I/he/she brought home the best report card ever.
- I was fearful as I walked up to the spooky house.
- I was angry when I found out my brother/sister had ruined my valuable _____ (cell phone, iPod, etc.) in the washing machine.
- I was sad at the end of the tearjerker movie.
- I walked into the surprise party, and was, of course, surprised.
- I was disgusted by the horrible meal I got at the Road Kill Café.
- I got frustrated looking for my lost homework.

Also be sure to tell students that nothing in particular needs to happen in these little scenes. They have a tendency to make something jump out of the spooky house, for instance, and chop the narrator's head off. That isn't the point. The point is to create suspense. Take us from the sidewalk to the front door, and show us how nervous the student with the bad report card is. Likewise, the point of the scenario with the angry sibling in the laundry room is not to have a narrator pounding on a sibling, but to show what he or she does immediately after finding the ruined object. Showing us the emotion makes any action that follows understandable.

# Audio Pictures—What People Say

Although the art of writing good dialogue is undervalued in schools, another way of showing what people are like is through their speech. As teaching the writing of fiction has been de-emphasized in schools, we tend to overlook how valuable dialogue can be in essay writing. Not only is dialogue writing fun, but it can also show us a lot about people, whether they are fictional or real, when it is carefully crafted.

## Overheard Conversations

Before I ask students to write dialogue, I ask them to read examples of good dialogue writing so they can get a sense of how it's written, and how it's formatted. Students tend to have a very hard time formatting dialogue, but it is possible to get them doing it correctly. One of the best stories I've ever found for teaching characterization through dialogue is Shirley Jackson's "The Sneaker Crisis," which features a mid-1900s family of six involved in finding a sneaker belonging to the oldest boy, the oddly named Laurie.

Each family member's personality is clearly developed through his or her dialogue. When we read the story aloud, I ask students to write down each character's personality as he or she is introduced.

The mother, who narrates, is always feeling martyred. "If you'd put things away neatly when you take them off instead of always throwing things under your bed—".

The son, Laurie, is an overdramatic teenage boy who is consistently judged as "rude" by my students. When his mother asks him if he's looked outside, he answers, "Now what would my sneaker be doing outdoors, I ask you? You think maybe I get dressed and undressed out on the lawn, maybe, for the neighbors?"

The older daughter, Janie, is, in the words of one of my students, "an 'emo' bookworm." She is crying, and the mother asks her if she's been reading *Little Women* again. Janie sniffles and says, "Just the part where Beth dies."

Sally and Barry, the five-year-old twins, have lines such as "I did unsee Laurie's sneaker a day and a day and a day and a day and many mornings ago," that prompt students to infer that the twins are "a little insane."

They quickly realize that not only is dialogue fun, but it also establishes character. I challenge students to find great passages of dialogue from the books they are reading and to share them in class.

## Principles of Dialogue Writing

I have tried writing extensive notes about how to format dialogue, all to no avail. It takes longer to tell about it than it does to show it (appropriately for this book). Here are my notes on dialogue as I present them to the class. There is only one rule worth writing out: *Indent each time the speaker changes.* For the rest, I simply show the rules underlying the following dialogue:

| Dialogue | Format |
|---|---|
| "Hello there, Cliff," said Buffy. | "Quote," said phrase. |
| Cliff said, "Hello there, Buffy." | Phrase said, "Quote." |
| "I think we should go out tonight," said Buffy. "I'm hungry." | "Sentence quote," said phrase. "2nd sentence quote." |
| "How about going to the Road Kill Café?" asked Cliff. | "Question quote?" said phrase. |
| "Well, now that you mention it," replied Buffy, "that sounds great!" | "Beginning of sentence quote," said phrase, "end of sentence quote." |
| "Let's go!" | "Quote!" [No said phrase, because the identity of the speaker is obvious.] |

## Flash Fiction—Dialogue

Dialogue can seem hard for students to master, but what is really needed are some quick practice exercises and a fast trip around the room to spot-check students to see if they are following the rules as posted. One thing I always do for starters is an activity with comic strips. I either copy some of my own, or save up some funnies pages from the newspaper. When I give the students a page of funnies, I tell them they must pick a strip with at least four "speech bubbles" back and forth between characters. I then tell them to rewrite the comic strip as a very, very short story. I tell them the names of the characters, or tell them to make up names if I don't know them. And, most important of all, I tell them to put in quotes anything that appears in bubbles. I encourage them to try out each of the formats on the chart above.

The great thing about this activity is that the students don't need to *create* dialogue. They merely need to *format* it. As students write, I circulate the room quickly, checking to see how they are doing and pointing out their mistakes. They can adjust quickly, make the correction, and then keep going. As students finish this activity, I let them look over each other's papers as well to check the formatting. We then move on to some activities that require them to actually make up the dialogue. We also discuss the fact that authors not only vary where the "said phrase" goes on a given line of dialogue, but they also sometimes leave out the "said phrase" all together. If just two characters are talking, they don't need to be identified every time they speak. But you do need to identify them often enough that the reader never has to count back up to the last "said phrase" and back down again (character A, character B, character A . . .) to figure out who's talking.

Keeping in mind that middle schoolers find the weird and dramatic quite engaging, I offer each of the following topics for them to try their dialogue-writing skills. For each one of these topics, I ask students to write down a personality for each character before they write, and keep in mind that they are writing their dialogue, in part, to help create and convey the characters' personalities.

1. *Ben Bunny tried to convince Freddy Fox not to eat him.*

This topic is a bit like a demented children's book gone wrong. Students usually jump right into it. I tell them it's up to them how it ends, but that the two characters should have distinctive personalities.

2. *Brad and Janet argued over his flirting with Gloria.*

As I said, students love drama. If Brad is dopey and Janet is jealous, so much the better. They usually have a great time creating a little soap opera. One note—I always announce that there is to be no physical violence in the scene, only bickering. I find it sad that I have to make this announcement, but I usually get such good writing from students with this scene that it's worth having to make the announcement.

3. *I tried to talk on the phone with my friend while my mom yelled at me to get off and go do my chores.*

The challenge here is to have a three-way conversation going on. They need to work at making it clear who is speaking on a given line. This scene is apparently duplicated in households all over the land, because students usually write very convincing dialogue. The mom's lines often end up being written in all capitals.

# Describing People in Essays

The uses for dialogue writing are obvious in fiction, but dialogue is often overlooked as a tool for essay writing. But think of almost any situation your students might write about in an essay, clichéd or not, and there is probably a way to include dialogue. It's especially useful as a grabber. Imagine the discussions students could record that would introduce topics such as gum chewing, dress code, or snacks in class (to name just a few clichéd topics).

*"Are you chewing gum, young lady?"*
*"Maybe . . ."*
*"Are you?"*
*"Well, yeah, but . . ."*
*"Throw it out, young lady!" the teacher says sternly, pointing at the trash.*
*"But I just put it in! The flavor's still fresh!"*
*How many times have you had to listen to exchanges like that in class? A waste of everybody's time, aren't they?*

With a one-sentence transition, you've moved from dialogue to the main part of your essay, but you've introduced your topic with a scene a reader can picture, and relate to.

Describing how people look, how they act and react to situations, and how they feel about things that are happening around them are all useful tools when explaining something or persuading people to take your point of view. Describing people and using dialogue aren't just useful for fiction. Students can describe how students, parents, and teachers would react to changes in policy at their school. They can describe how people would react to changes in their community, their state, their country, their world. They can go beyond telling us how people feel. They can *show* us their reactions, their emotions, and their conversations—the bad, but also the good.

# Pictures in Action: Moment-by-Moment Narration

As I mentioned in the Introduction, I once tried to get my tenth graders to try their hand at some fiction writing. One of the stories I received read something like this:

*There was this spaceship, and it landed on a planet. Two guys came out and these big aliens came and ripped their heads off, and there was blood everywhere. They died.*

Okay, maybe it was longer than that, but it wasn't *much* longer. And what bothered me here wasn't so much the blatant obviousness of the final sentence, which implies the "guys" could get their heads ripped off and *not* die, but the complete lack of suspense, the failure to put the reader in the scene, and the absence of any attempt to make us *care*.

After reading this story—and about seventy more like it—I invented two terms that I have taught ever since: list-of-events narration and moment-by-moment narration. It's not that one is bad and the other is good necessarily, but that the two types of narration are good for different things. The story above was written as list-of-events narration, but it should have been written as moment-by-moment narration. On the other hand, if the story had started on Earth, and it had taken several months or years for the guys to get to Planet Headrip, then list-of-events narration would have been fine to describe that journey. "They ate, slept, and played gin rummy all the way to Planet Headrip." We don't need to know much about the trip.

Moment-by-moment narration, on the other hand, implies that you are putting us in the scene, giving us the experience. I explain that Stephen King is not one of the world's best-selling authors just because he's gory, but because he takes the time to create characters we care about (see Chapters 5 and 6), and then he puts them in awful situations, which he describes in such a way that we feel as if we are there. Other authors put their characters in funny situations instead—but they still use moment-by-moment narration to make the situations come to life.

Before I go any further, let me emphasize that moment-by-moment narration is by no means limited to fiction, or even to narrative nonfiction. It is an effective tool to use in any kind of writing, and we'll discuss how to use it later—including in comparative, expository, and persuasive essays. But before you can use a technique effectively, you have to practice it.

# Examples from Literature: Comparing Narrative Styles

List-of-events narration is not always bad; in fact it's often essential. In a novel, to have to follow characters through every single thing they do might be deadly dull, depending on the story. The example I often discuss with students is the Harry Potter books. Each book takes place over a year of fictitious time, so to go into moment-by-moment detail would get extremely tedious. J. K. Rowling uses moment-by-moment narration for big events, turning points in the plot where she wants to make us feel that we are *there*.

But in between those major events, she has a lot of list-of-events narration, like this pastiche sentence I constructed based on many similar ones from the books: "Weeks passed. Harry was still being tormented by rumors about him that were circulating the campus, and Ron and Hermione were still quarrelling about something or other to hide their true feelings about each other." If she hadn't used this type of narration, the series would have been around 8,000 pages long instead of merely in the range of 4,000. Each book covers only a year of fictitious action, yet book one is 309 pages long and book five is 870. The difference? The longer books have a greater number of important moment-by-moment events, and probably fewer list-of-events jumps between major sequences.

When we read stories in class, I often ask students to observe where and why the two types of narration are used—and how they are used.

## Narrative Example: *Banner in the Sky*

John Ramsey Ullman's novel *Banner in the Sky*, about an aspiring mountain climber named Rudi, has often had its second chapter, "A Boy and a Man," excerpted as a short story in literature anthologies. In the chapter, Rudi is hiking across an alpine glacier and finds that a man has fallen into a deep gorge in the ice, gotten stuck on a ledge, and can't climb the overhanging, slippery walls. If night falls, he will surely freeze to death, and there is not enough daylight left to go get help. Rudi, risking his own life, makes a lifeline out of his walking stick, his jacket, and nearly all his clothes. He lays across the ice nearly naked, the cold burning into his skin, and lowers the staff to the man below, who begins to climb. What follows is as good an example of moment-by-moment narration as I have ever read:

He braced himself. The pull came. His toes went taut in their ice-holds, and his hands tightened on the staff until the knuckles showed white. Again he could hear a scraping sound below, and he knew that the man was clawing his boots against the ice wall, trying both to lever himself up and take as much weight as possible off the improvised lifeline. But the wall obviously offered little help. Almost all his weight was on the lifeline. Suddenly there was a jerk, as one of the knots in the clothing slipped, and the staff was almost wrenched from Rudi's hands. But the knot held. And his hands held. He tried to call down, "All right?" but he had no breath for words. From below, the only sound was the scraping of boots on ice.

How long it went on Rudi could never have said. Perhaps only a minute or two. But it seemed like hours. And then at last—it happened. A hand came into view around the curve of the crevasse wall: a hand gripping the twisted fabric of his jacket, and then a second hand rising slowly above it. A head appeared. A pair of shoulders. A face was raised for an instant and then lowered. Again one hand moved slowly past the other.

But Rudi no longer saw it, for now his eyes were shut tight with the strain. His teeth were clamped, the cords of his neck bulged, the muscles of his arm felt as if he were being drawn one by one from the bones that held them. He began to lose his toe-holds. He was being dragged forward. Desperately, frantically, he dug in with his feet, pressed his whole body down, as if he could make it part of the glacier. Though all but naked on the ice, he was pouring with sweat. Somehow he stopped the slipping. Somehow he held on. But now suddenly the strain was even worse, for the man had reached the lower end of the staff. The slight "give" of the stretched clothing was gone, and in its place was rigid deadweight on a length of wood. The climber was close now. But heavy. Indescribably heavy. Rudi's hands ached and burned, as if it were a rod of hot lead that they clung to. It was not a mere man that he was holding, but a giant; or a block of granite. The pull was unendurable. The pain was unendurable. He could hold on no longer. His hands were opening. It was all over (pp. 26–27).

It is all over because the man has scrambled to the top.

We read this scene aloud in class twice—once to be immersed in the story (students usually tell me they feel their own muscles tensing as we read it), and once to analyze what makes it work so well. After we have read it once, we discuss how the scene would have read as "list-of-events" narration. The class usually comes up with something like this: "Rudi lowered the makeshift lifeline, and it hurt really bad, and the guy was really heavy, and it felt like hours, but the man finally reached the top." The contrast between the two narrative styles couldn't be plainer.

In order to look at what makes the scene work, we list the chief ingredient of moment-by-moment narration—our old friends, strong verbs. I note that Ullman has plenty of dead verbs and even some adjectives in this scene, but they are nearly always linked to or followed by strong verbs or figurative language. The list of verbs ends up looking like this: *braced, went taut, tightened, showed, could hear, clawing, lever, offered, slipped, wrenched, held, gripping, rising, appeared, raised, lowered, moved, saw, were shut tight, were clamped, bulged, felt, drawn, began to lose, being dragged, dug, pressed, pouring, stopped, slipping, held, reached, ached, burned, clung to, opening.*

The act of listing these verbs from moment-by-moment narration students have read is important, because when they move on to writing their own moment-by-moment narration, they will start by creating a similar list of verbs. There are places where Ullman uses list-of-events narration to move over action quickly when necessary. As Rudi and the man head back to town they talk, but then, "they moved on without speaking. It was now late afternoon, and behind them the stillness was broken by a great roaring, as sun-loosened rock and ice broke off from the heights of the Citadel. When they reached the path, Rudi spoke again, hesitantly" (p. 34). Ullman describes the avalanche, and suddenly they have reached the path into town. We didn't need a moment-by-moment description of the two of them walking down the path for a couple of hours.

## Narrative Example: *Making My Escape*

In my novel *Making My Escape*, I used similar techniques to make a harrowing scene come to life. Daniel Finn, his mother, and his sister are trying to escape an alcoholic father's drunken rage by taking the car he has forbidden them to leave in. The father has gone back in the house, and the other three family members are sneaking around his work garage and back to the family garage where the car is sitting. Daniel narrates. Note the emphasis on strong verbs, which I've underlined in the excerpt.

"Where are we going, Mommy?" Laura asked.

"We're circling around the gray garage and back to the driveway. We're taking the car."

Whatever else you could say about my mother, she was persistent. When we reached the back of the gray garage, we stopped and looked across the lawn and the driveway to the house. Dad wasn't on the back steps or porch, and although all the lights were on in the kitchen, he wasn't there either. My mother led us quietly, but quickly across the lawn and over to the car. She opened her door very quietly and put her finger to her lips to tell me to do the same. Laura crawled into the back seat. Mom whispered, "Don't slam the doors all the way until I've got the engine started and we're moving." She put the key in the ignition, and then looked at it before she turned it as if to say 'come on, engine, turn over for me.' She turned the key. The engine came on immediately. She immediately shifted into reverse and started backing up so quickly I thought we might fly off the hill.

The back door flew open and my father came bounding out into the bright glow of the headlights. He ran down the driveway toward us, covering the whole distance in what looked like five strides. We had backed out and were about to head down the street, when my father appeared in the headlights right in front of the car, his face under-lit by the headlights, cast in strange surreal shadows like a character in an old horror movie. But this was much scarier. He yelled at us—I don't remember what he yelled—and for a moment I thought my mom might run him over out of sheer surprise or terror. The next moment, he was diving to the driver's side door, and we both remembered to slam our doors all the way closed at that moment. My father stood by the side of the door, shaking the car. I never knew if he was trying to take the door off with his bare hands or tip us over, but the next moment we were speeding down the road, leaving him literally in the dust (pp. 220–222).

If you can get copies made of a text or section of text containing moment-by-moment narration, asking students to underline or highlight the words can help point out how much they influence the "feel" of a scene and make it vivid to a reader.

# Creating Moment-by-Moment Narration: The Mad Dash

After we've read some examples of moment-by-moment narration, I introduce writing it by using a writing exercise I call "The Mad Dash." I write the following topic sentence on the board: "I made a mad dash to get to class on time." I tell students that they are limited to the four minutes between classes and must describe those four minutes moment-by-moment, like a movie, showing us exactly what's going on. What I like about this scenario is the time limitation. Whatever is going to happen can only take a few minutes—it focuses students. There is almost no room to be vague. I tell them that this is a piece of fiction, but that they can use things that have really happened to them. It may be that they have two tardies to class already, and one more gets them written up and also grounded at home, thus adding to the desperation. The object is to throw as many obstacles in their narrator's way as possible. It is entirely up to them whether they make it to class on time or not, or whether they decide to have a twist ending. I tell them to make it a worst-case scenario.

*Chapter 7: Pictures in Action: Moment-by-Moment Narration*

## Strong Verbs

Strong verbs are the backbone of moment-by-moment narration, and so before students start writing "The Mad Dash," I have them brainstorm some verbs—actions their narrator can take in their effort to get to class. I write them on the board, but I ask the students to write them in the margins of their paper, or on a separate prewrite page. I start by writing the obvious *dashed*, then add *ran*. Students then begin calling out their suggestions, which I write on the board as fast as I can. Usually the list includes words like *crashed*, *jumped*, *twisted*, *turned*, *kicked*, *jogged*, *slammed*, *tripped*, *fell*, *bumped*, *leaped*, *ducked*, *dodged*, *pushed*, *pulled*, *squeezed*, *bounced*, *jostled*, *trampled*, *bashed*, *whirled*, *spun*, *grabbed*, *limped*, *galloped*, *avoided*, *sneaked*, and *skidded out*. Are there more? Sure! See what your students come up with.

Once this list is on the board, and on their papers, I let students know that it's a resource, not a checklist. They don't have to use all of those words, and certainly not in that order. What's important is that their paragraphs are is filled with specific *actions*.

## Concrete Nouns

These actions need to be set in the hallways at your school, hallways filled with people and objects. Our next step before writing is to come up with a list of people, places, and objects who might figure into their four-minute epic.

Characters in this scenario will be the kinds of people who will serve as obstacles or threats to the narrator's completing his or her mission. They might include their own friends. Custodians, maintenance people, and groundskeepers might also figure into the mix. They might include administrators—my students usually include Mr. Strother, our ex-Marine assistant principal in charge of discipline. I ask them to think about places they might need to stop—their locker, the bathroom.

A note about the bathroom—I tell students they should take their narrators to the door, and then have them come back out. We really don't need to follow the narrative into the bathroom—there is such a thing as too much detail!

Brainstorming a list of things that they might run into, we usually start with backpacks and then move on to other objects and obstacles students might encounter in their mad dash to class. The list often includes items such as sneakers, combination locks, door handles, sidewalks, cracks in the sidewalks, stairs, carts, golf carts, pillars, grass, flowers, books, notebooks, signs, elevators, walls, ceilings, courtyards, chairs, groups, fights, kissing couples, garbage cans, and opening doors.

## Sensory Detail and Description

Moment-by-moment narrative needs to take place in a . . . place. So description, which we've already discussed elsewhere, figures into what we're doing. If our narrator is going to run down a narrow hall, we need to describe the hall. Sensory detail can come into play as well, especially if your narrator crashes into and tips over an over-full and over-ripe garbage can. What does it smell like? How is your narrator feeling during the run to class? So as a last bit of prewriting, I ask them to think about what sensory detail they can include as they write. Sight is a given, and taste rarely comes into play for this topic, so I ask them to concentrate on sound, smell, and touch.

Once again, we do a quick brainstorm. Sounds can include adults yelling, students screaming, feet pounding, lockers slamming, late bells ringing, and classroom doors slamming shut. Smells could include body odors, garbage smells, and the scent of fresh-cut grass (as your narrator leaps over the mower). Your narrator can feel his heart pounding, his pulse filling up his ears, his sweaty hands.

## The Mad Dash Paragraph

By the time you have finished brainstorming as a class, your students will have too many details to pack into a four-minute "word movie." They will have to pick and choose and rearrange and combine to make even some of it fit. I usually give students 10 to 15 minutes to craft their narratives. They can use or not use the items in the group brainstorm, and they can certainly add details of their own invention. The purpose of the prewrite is twofold: to show them the kinds of details moment-by-moment narration should have, and to show them how easy it is to generate a lot of ideas fast.

We also talk about twist endings. It is up to each writer whether the student arrives on time or is late and gets punished, but I tell them that there are other options if they can think of them. One of the most popular endings involves arriving on time only to find a sign on the door saying the class is meeting in the Media Center that day.

After students finish writing, I ask them to exchange papers and underline their best or funniest moments within the piece. The paragraphs are all pretty consistently funny. What I then emphasize to students is that these same principles of strong verbs, concrete nouns, and sensory detail apply whenever you are trying to put your reader into a scene moment by moment. They won't always have to brainstorm extensively as long as they keep those things in mind, and having gone through an exercise like this one will make an impression. Their perception of what it means to narrate a scene will change.

# Moment-by-Moment Exercises

The following exercises can be used with the prewriting technique listed above, with some parts of it, or without prewriting at all. What you care about is whether students are using the kinds of strong verbs, concrete nouns, and sensory details that will make the scene come alive on the page. The first prompts are more specific, but toward the end of the list they are more open-ended, allowing the student writer to supply the specifics.

| PROMPTS FOR MOMENT-BY-MOMENT NARRATION | |
|---|---|
| I tried to sneak past my parents. | I *had* to win. |
| I was being followed. | It was out of control. |
| I climbed as fast as I could. | It was total chaos. |
| I searched frantically. | I hung on for dear life. |
| I knew I was lost. | I tried to stop it from happening. |

# Using Moment-by-Moment Narration in Nonfiction

It goes without saying that this type of narration is useful in fiction, but I ask students to think as they write: Does a given event need moment-by-moment treatment, or can it be glossed over with a list-of-events treatment? Most stories, especially slightly longer ones, will have both kinds of narration.

This technique may appear to be useful only in fiction, but nonfiction, even persuasive and expository nonfiction, can utilize narrative techniques successfully. The new classification of creative nonfiction has caught on, and nonfiction pieces are now being written using fiction writing techniques and narrative styles. Using moment-by-moment narration can help add life to almost any essay. Here are several ways moment-by-moment narration can be used in nonfiction.

## As a Grabber or Clincher

A nonfiction essay is, by definition, about real life. And real life is made up of moments. Almost any problem or situation you wish to address in an essay can be framed in terms of a specific moment. Write a scene depicting the embarrassment of being called out on a dress code violation. Write a specific scene showing everyone sitting in the auditorium being lectured as punishment for the misbehavior of a few people. Write a specific scene that gives readers your particular window into a bigger problem. A kayak trip ruined by a bunch of litter in the stream is a great way into the topic of pollution. As always, you can exit as you entered an essay—by creating a parallel but different scene. Show the results of a change—a clean river to kayak down, for instance.

## As a Narrative "Thread" That Flows Through an Essay

In the emerging form of creative nonfiction, a nonnarrative essay may incorporate narrative elements. When my son wrote an essay on the rather bizarre topic, "The Pirates Versus the Ninjas," he interspersed his analysis of which group would win in a fight with scenes of a fictitious battle that demonstrated the points he made. An essay about something that affects students throughout the school day, like a too-short class-change, might have little bits of the "mad dash" sprinkled throughout it to demonstrate how hard it is to get class on time, even when you're trying.

## As a Means of Making Hypothetical Situations Vivid

Chapter 8, "Pictures of Situations," addresses this topic in more detail, but it's worth noting that many non-fiction essays, especially persuasive pieces, ask the reader to imagine what might happen if different scenarios come to pass. Moment-by-moment narration can make these scenes vivid, whether the writer is describing a problem, a solution, or the potential effects of a policy.

## As Comparison/Contrast

If you are organizing an essay around two contrasting viewpoints, options, or ideas, using a pair of contrasting narratives throughout the essay can help highlight differences. For instance, if you are comparing dropping out versus staying in school, it is one thing to give us facts and statistics about the benefits and consequences of the two choices. It's another thing entirely to give us short, pointed narratives about a dropout and a graduate that show us, rather than tell us, what those consequences are.

## As Personal Experience

If you have been affected by a policy, then telling your story may be one of the best persuasive techniques you have for changing people's minds. If something bad and/or annoying has happened to you that relates to your topic, use that experience in your essay. An essay about rudeness that quotes statistics from studies on public manners won't hold a candle to an essay filled with vivid moment-by-moment narration about rude cell-phone talkers, graduation goers, movie interrupters, or line-butters.

# The Merits of Narrative

We ask students to write essays that are not narrative, I suppose, because abstract thought is seen as more rigorous and challenging than telling stories. Maybe it is. But the best presenters of abstract thought, be they science writers, philosophers, or theologians, know that the most effective way to make people understand abstract concepts is to tell stores that make them concrete. I've read that narrative is the oldest form of human communication, and as such it holds a deep, almost primal power over our minds. Why not let our students, and ourselves, use that hold to our advantage, no matter what kind of writing we are doing?

# Pictures of Situations: Hypothetical Scenarios

**A**s of this writing, the news is filled with debates about health care in the United States. How can we provide it for everyone without ruining it for anyone? To what extent should the government be involved? As with any issue, I've been reading editorials and newspaper columns, and, as always, I'm listening not only to the substance of people's arguments, but also to the methods they use to argue.

Those in favor of universal health care reform paint a picture of what it could be like in the future—quality low-cost health care for all. Those opposed to universal health care paint a different picture—low quality, inefficient, government-run health care that leaves people waiting months for even the simplest of procedures. By the time this book goes to press, some kind of compromise will have been reached, but what interests me in the here and now is the method of argument being used. People on both sides of the issues are "painting pictures" of the future. I call those pictures "hypothetical situations."

For our students, the major pitfall of nonfiction essay writing is that, unlike concrete-event-filled narratives, nonfiction writing is about abstract ideas—the goodness and badness of things. And because essays are about abstract ideas, students tend to write about them in abstract ways, mainly by using adjectives. Gum chewing rules are bad! Vending machines are good! School uniforms are bad! Freedom of expression is good!

But students often feel there's no story to tell, no narrative technique to make the ideas vivid.

Hypothetical scenarios ask "What if?" and allow students to inject a little science fiction writing, that most exotic of fictional forms, right into their nonfiction essay. What is science fiction, after all, but answering big "What if?" questions in a concrete way?

Lois Lowry asks, "What if we created a society where we tried to avoid all pain?" The result is *The Giver*. Ray Bradbury asks, "What would society be like if everyone gave up reading books?" The result is *Fahrenheit 451*. George Orwell asks, "What if there were no privacy, and the government was allowed to watch your activities 24/7?" The result is *1984*.

Those are hypothetical scenarios on a grand scale. But when our students write essays, they can create the same effect on a smaller scale. Want to show us what life would be like without a no-gum-chewing rule, or with school uniforms or vending machines? By using a hypothetical scenario, you can take us into the future and create the scene.

It is too easy to say, "Everyone will be happy," or "Everyone will be unhappy," in a certain circumstance. It is far better to show us a scene—what will the future actually look like? This chapter will present ways to imagine and present alternate futures to make your point of view look good and your opponent's look undesirable.

Hypothetical scenarios can use all of the tools I've described in this book so far: moment-by-moment narration, descriptions of places and people, movie techniques, and sensory detail. It's how the scenarios are used that I'll be discussing here, and how those scenarios, in turn, use all the other techniques we've been discussing.

## Types of Scenarios

Most persuasive essays are about change—either preventing it or wanting it to happen. So if you want to *create* change, you first want to show how bad things are now. This isn't hard—you just describe things as they are now, assuming you think they're bad. You then want to show us how great things will be in the future.

On the other hand, if you want to *prevent* change, you must describe how good things are now—again not really hard since what we're describing is already there—and then show how bad things *could* get in the future.

For instance, look at the gum-chewing rule in schools. I know that this is a clichéd topic, perhaps the *ultimate* clichéd topic, but using it helps us demonstrate how this technique can add new life to even the dullest of subjects. At any rate, right now we are banning gum, so we can show how awful the ban is. Students chew gum anyway because it helps them concentrate, so the ban is ineffective. They have to hide the gum, so it gets stuck everywhere. The teachers and administrators have to waste time dealing with gum as a discipline issue. We have a lot of issues with the gum-chewing rule, all of which can be elaborated on—more on this subject later.

I ask my students to brainstorm: how *could* it be if the rule were changed? Well, if students were allowed to chew gum, the students would be happier, and happier with the adults at school. Because there would be no need to hide the gum, students wouldn't be sticking it all over campus where it often gets underfoot—literally. And there would be fewer discipline issues, leaving adults free to deal with really important discipline issues—and to chew gum themselves if they so desire. Everyone is happy. These results of changing the gum rule are the stuff hypothetical scenarios are made of. Again, more on how to develop these scenarios shortly.

Keep in mind, though, that the technique could be used in reverse for this topic. I've found a surprising number of students who are in favor of the gum ban. Their take on the subject could be to show us that right now the gum ban is working, and that the hypothetical lifting of the ban would be a disaster. We brainstorm what that would be like as well. Gum would be even more in evidence all over campus. Students would chew loudly in class and pass gum around to share, distracting others. And when gum did create a distraction, teachers would have to just put up with it. Different scenario—this time showing us how bad lifting the gum ban would be.

When we are discussing this concept in class and students are adding it to their writers' notebooks, we show it like this:

| To create change: | To prevent change: |
| --- | --- |
| Show us how things are BAD NOW. | Show us how things are GREAT NOW. |
| Show us how things COULD BE GREAT. | Show us how things COULD BE BAD. |

This setup can, in fact, be used as a way to organize a persuasive essay as a comparison-contrast. But once a student has decided *what* he is going to show us, he has to decide *how* to show us.

# Elaborating Scenarios

For any given change, there are several possible ways that the potential hazards and benefits of the change could be shown in an essay. How would the change influence a place, a person, a group, an object, or an event or set of events? When I introduce this concept, I use the gum-chewing topic as an exercise—that way they never actually have to write a whole essay about it.

## Showing Hypothetical Settings

Many changes will affect places. Gum chewing, for instance, can affect nearly every location on a campus. If we blame the ban for the fact that gum is stuck all over campus, we can describe the school with gum stuck all over the place. If we say the problem will grow worse if the ban is lifted, then we still get to have the fun of describing the school with gum stuck all over the place. Both sides agree on the problem; they merely disagree on its causes—a rhetorical fact worth noting. Building on our lessons about describing places earlier, we can brainstorm all the places gum can be stuck—and what verbs will describe how it is stuck there.

Again we brainstorm as a class. Where and how could gum be stuck?

| Where could gum get stuck? | How could gum get stuck (verbs)? |
| --- | --- |
| Under desks | rammed |
| On the floor | stuck |
| On the sidewalks | dropped |
| On walls | plastered |
| In textbooks | squished |
| Under bookshelves | pressed |
| In lockers | pushed |
| Under seats | deposited |
| On book bags | stowed away |

Brainstorm with the class how the setting might be described in terms of movies shots. From a long shot, maybe the problem is invisible. But at a medium shot, you can start to see floors and sidewalks speckled with ugly globs of old gum. In close-up shots you can see the gum stuck under desks, chairs, shelves . . . all the places listed above.

Also note that sensory detail can come into this scene—especially the sense of touch. Ask students to describe what it feels like to step in gum, or touch it. How does old, hard gum differ from gum that has been freshly chewed? Disgusting to ponder, but also vivid!

Gum-chewing policy is one example, but so are other, more significant changes. Skateboarding laws downtown (a favorite of many of my male students), the absence or presence of a community teen center, or lawn ordinances are also possibilities. I often start our discussion about hypothetical places by having students brainstorm changes that would affect various places. The lists sometimes look like these:

## Changes that would affect a school:

- Allowing students to paint murals on the walls
- Changing the landscaping of a public area
- Allowing teachers to choose their own classroom paint-color schemes
- Having campus advisors who would only monitor bathrooms
- Adding (or removing) security cameras
- De-emphasizing standardized testing—what would classrooms look like?

## Changes that would affect a community:

- Having every street be "adopted" by an individual, neighborhood group, or organization
- Having a teen center
- Allowing teenagers to create murals to discourage graffiti (on public buildings?)
- Stopping public events like art festivals and parades because of the high cost of after-event clean-up
- Having bike trails and lanes available
- Having "red-light cameras" to catch red-light runners at intersections

## Changes that might affect your state or country:

- Encouraging alternative energy sources
- Fully funding education vs. cutting education budgets
- Cracking down on underage drinking
- Discouraging gangs

## Changes that might affect the world:

- Changing policies that affect the environment
- Attempting different ways to deal with terrorism
- Breaking down cultural barriers via the Internet
- Stopping pollution

It goes beyond the main focus of this book to get into a major discussion of how to generate topics. I will say, however, that many of the writing prompts, like the standard "gum" prompt, are much better used as examples and exercises than actual topics for assignments. For real assignments, I try to trust that my students have things to say—it's my job to help them find those things, not to supply them with easy, canned topics.

Showing changes in a place is one type of hypothetical scenario—but changes in a place matter because of how they affect people.

## Exercises for Showing Hypothetical Settings:

- Show the cafeteria with different food choices.
- Show classrooms with huge classroom libraries instead of textbooks.
- Show the school with a different schedule.
- Show what it would be like if cell phones were allowed all day long at school.
- Show the town with more bike trails and walking trails.
- Show the state's schools without standardized tests!

## Showing a Person

Some persuasive essays are of a personal nature—you are actually persuading the reader to make a personal change, for example, persuading the reader to change a habit, to do something positive, to avoid doing something bad. The old standby topic of "Persuade your friend to not drop out of school" falls into this category.

As an exercise, I ask students to create a picture of a young person who has dropped out versus one who has stayed in school. This picture often includes not only what the person is doing in terms of jobs and education (or lack thereof), but also how they dress (bargain basement vs. brand name), where they live, who they hang out with, and how they feel. By the time a student has described all of those aspects of the person's life, he or she will have a section of essay writing packed with word pictures that show the reader why it's important to stay in school.

Whenever you discuss any kind of change, it is good to bring it down to one hypothetical person who will be affected by that change. When students create such a hypothetical person, they should consider how the change will affect him or her in the following areas:

- physical appearance
- living conditions
- working conditions
- social life
- emotional life

All of these aspects can be shown using tools we've already discussed to describe settings, appearances, behaviors, and emotions.

### Exercises for Showing a Person

- Show a student who goes from unorganized to organized.
- Show how changing your attitude can change your relationships.
- Show how lack of education can have long-term effects on a person's life and health.
- Show how alcohol or substance abuse can affect a person's health.
- Show how having goals can transform a person's life.
- Show how important exercise can be to a person's health.

## Showing a Group

In *Writing Extraordinary Essays* (Scholastic, 2008), I discuss different organizational patterns for essays, and one of those patterns is "Affected People"—building an entire essay around how something will affect different groups. Any change a student might be writing persuasively about will affect various groups of people.

Any change at school has the potential to affect teachers, students, administrators, parents, other staff members, and possibly the community at large. Any change in a community could affect various groups within the community—different age groups, different types of business people, different types of residents. Any change in society at large can have ripple effects on many different groups. I emphasize to my students that they must show us how different types of people will have to act and react differently, depending on the changes being argued about.

I return just one more time to the gum topic, simply because it fits this type of word picture so beautifully. How would allowing gum affect students, teachers, administrators, and custodians? Well, it depends on whether you think gum should be banned or allowed. Or does it? We'll look at one group. If you think the gum ban is what makes people hide gum, then you could show us happy custodians who no longer have to scrape gum off sidewalks and now have time to water the plants and put fresh coats of paint around the school. On the other hand, if you think allowing gum will just make the problem worse, you can show unhappy custodians scraping gum from sidewalks and the undersides of desks while the plants wither and the paint peels.

The important thing is to show us what members of a group will be *doing* if something changes, not just how they'll *feel*.

### Exercises for Showing a Group

- Show how eliminating arts education would affect artists, theater students, or musicians.
- Show how making high school athletes pay fees to play sports would affect low-income students.
- Explain how giving each student a laptop might affect student learning.
- Explain how smaller class sizes might affect student learning.
- Explain how a strict curfew might affect students or parents.

## Showing a Change in Society or the World

Of all the things I find most worrisome in society right now, the one that strikes closest to home with me is the potential (some say inevitable) demise of the newspaper. I'm afraid that someday my only source of news will be the Internet, which chooses for its big headlines stories about vapid celebrities and wrinkle creams. I know our newspaper journalists aren't perfect, but they operate in a different way than your average blogger. Without newspapers, who will get paid to report news? If no one is getting paid, will anyone bother to report it? Local reporting in particular is likely to go away almost completely.

Simply by talking about the topic, I've started projecting into the future—a world without newspapers.

Showing a change in society is the closest we'll come to writing pure science fiction within an essay. When we ask students to consider a change in society or the world, we're really asking them to describe a very large group of individual people.

There are several ways of describing a changed society. Students can describe a society in any of these terms:

- your average person
- people
- everyone
- no one
- they

I recently reread *Fahrenheit 451* with my eighth graders and was struck by how the society is described by those very terms. Society is a great, faceless entity in the book, but Bradbury shows us that entity doing very specific things. Clarisse, the voice of reason in the book, talks of how "everyone I know is either shouting or dancing around like wild or beating up on each other. Do you notice how people hurt each other nowadays" (p. 30)?

Later, the voice of evil in the novel, the book-burning Captain Beatty, describes society this way: "Give people contests they win by remembering the words to the more popular songs, or the names of the state capitals, or how much corn Iowa grew last year" (p. 61).

Instead of showing what a person will do if society changes, it is possible to show what *people* will do. I tell students their job is to create images similar to the planet Camazotz in *A Wrinkle in Time*, where every household does exactly the same things all day long. I tell them to write about large groups doing things as a single entity.

### Exercises for Showing a Change in Society or the World

- Show how the Internet will make everyone either more or less literate.
- Show what would happen if we stopped forcing kids to come to school.
- Show what would happen if we made college free to anyone.
- Show what would happen if we made guns easier/harder to get.
- Show what might happen if the Internet translated languages so that Facebook or MySpace could operate between cultures.
- Show what might happen if every country consumed materials and energy the way the United States does.
- Show what might happen if most Americans lived close enough to work to commute by bicycle.

## Showing an Event

Showing a single, representative event from the future can be a powerful tool for creating change. Look at the change the Ghost of Christmas Yet to Come accomplishes in Ebenezer Scrooge by showing him the future!

A specific event can be used to show a change in a place, a person, a group, or a society—or sometimes all of those things at once. Students can show the setting, or use camera angles, moment-by-moment narration, sensory details, dialogue, descriptions of emotions—nearly every trick in this book—to create a scene that shows us a change. Of course, the change can be positive or negative, depending on how students depict the scene.

Ask students to describe a graduation scene: the stadium, the crowds, the robes and mortarboards, the noisemakers, conversations, people's facial expressions. The scene takes on a different meaning depending on whether the subject of the essay is graduating with his peers or sitting in the crowd observing because he dropped out.

On a more futuristic societal note, you might warn against the demise of print and of handwriting by showing the moment in the future where all writing skills and printed media have vanished—and we suddenly run out of power. What then?

### Exercises for Showing an Event

- Show a person's graduation ceremony.
- Show someone's funeral.
- Show someone's wedding.
- Show an important announcement being made.
- Show an awards ceremony.
- Show a game-winning moment.
- Show a standing ovation.
- Show a scene of people enjoying something good.
- Show a scene of people suffering through something bad.

# What If?

Science fiction writers often ask "What if?" But asking "What if?" isn't just for science fiction. Our student essay writers can create alternate futures in their nonfiction essays. And once they've done it on a small scale, who knows? They might go on to write the next great American sci-fi novel.

# CHAPTER 9

# Pictures in Frames: Movie and Comic-Strip Techniques

As I noted in the introduction, many of our students are quite savvy about visuals. They watch movies, televisions shows, YouTube videos, music videos, and video games. They are awash in visuals, and yet they seem barely aware of how those visuals work in movies—or how they could be used in their own writing. This chapter will help your students start thinking about their writing in truly visual terms . . . as movies. All of the techniques film directors and cinematographers use are available to writers. We simply create our movies with words.

## Cinematic Concepts

When making a movie, comic strip, or comic book, an artist has a number of choices to make with each shot or frame. In his book *Making Comics*, Scott McCloud identifies those choices: subject, moment, frame, angle, lighting, and flow from one frame to the next. This chapter will help students think visually about their writing, viewing it as a movie they are creating rather than a series of facts and adjectives they are stringing together.

If you search for "cinematic terms" online, you will find a host of Web sites that will give you similar definitions for many of the terms used in moviemaking. Most of them will be too technical or specific to be useful to writers, so I've narrowed the list to the ones that student writers will find helpful.

### Camera Angles

This concept obviously refers to where the camera is placed when filming a scene. When students write, they don't have a literal camera, but they do have control of how their readers see things. This concept runs throughout this chapter—that we each have an imaginary camera in our heads, and we direct it in certain ways to make our readers see things the way we want them to be seen. We use our "cameras" in different ways to create different effects. (For a quick summary of these effects, see Figure 9-1, page 102.)

### Low angle:

*The camera is pointing up toward the subject, which can make it seem overpowering or menacing.*

If you watch any movie with a strong villain, that villain will often be filmed from a low angle to make him look taller. In an iconic scene in *Star Wars Episode V: The Empire Strikes Back*, Luke Skywalker approaches Darth Vader to duel with him. Luke is placed down low, while Vader is high up, making him look more intimidating. A low camera angle can also create a sense of wonder. In *E.T.: the Extraterrestrial*, Steven Spielberg opens the film with a scene of the little alien wandering through a forest. A low camera angle emphasizes not only E.T.'s diminutive size, but also his sense of wonder about the forest he's come to investigate. Of course, almost immediately, the low angle is used to create menace again, as government "alien hunters" arrive and are filmed from a low angle as they pursue E. T. through the forest.

### Straight On:

*The camera is at eye level with the subject being filmed (the most common angle).*

It is interesting that the most commonly used film technique in each category here (angle, frame, lighting) is the most neutral. Extremes are generally saved for more dramatic purposes. A straight-on camera angle lacks drama—it lets the action speak for itself. Something to note is that comedies and funny comic strips tend to use straight-on camera angles, because fancy angles would distract from the humor. Dramatic movies and superhero comic books tend to use more high- and low-angle shots to create dramatic effects. In terms of writing, straight-on shots are probably scenes the author would write about without commenting on the angle at all.

### High angle:

*The camera is high up, looking down on the subject of the frame, which can make the subject appear small or vulnerable.*

Going once again to a galaxy far, far away, when Darth Vader makes his entrance in *The Empire Strikes Back*, he passes by a group of his minions, Imperial officers, who are down in a pit on the bridge of his ship. The camera looks down at them, capturing their fearful faces as Vader passes. These techniques are used in animation as well. In *The Lion King*, when Simba discovers his father has died, he is shown from above, looking small and helpless as he calls for help.

## Lighting

Lighting, which includes shadowing, is extremely important in movies, comic books, and comic strips. It helps set the mood of the piece. Lighting effects can be created with words, and, as I'll demonstrate later, describing light and shadow can be useful even when writing nonfiction essays.

## Low key:

*Lighting is dim, emphasizing a contrast between light and shadows.*

Think film noir. Gaslight. Mystery. Magic. This kind of lighting can create all kinds of effects, and it works in films and comics. In the usually neutral-key comic strip *Calvin and Hobbes*, when Calvin daydreams that he's a private-eye, Tracer Bullet, the frames become filled with black-shadowed areas. Interestingly, low-key lighting can be used to create brooding, suspense-filled scenes (think *Psycho*), but also magical scenes (think, again, of *E.T.*).

## High key:

*Lighting is very bright and floods the picture.*

High-key lighting can be positive or negative, depending on how it's used. A day at the sea under a blue sky can create a very sunny, happy effect. A day in a sea of office cubicles under fluorescent lights can seem oppressive.

## Neutral key:

*Lighting is neutral, neither bright nor dark.*

Again, what is neutral on film probably won't find its way into writing. But it's worth noting nonetheless.

## Frames

I've saved the most important film concept for last: frames. Framing determines what we actually choose to focus on when we write. Framing, in fact, is what good writing, good art, is all about. In his book *Whistling in the Dark*, Frederick Buechner writes about a haiku and says that what the writer of the haiku is doing "is putting a frame around the moment" (p. 15). He talks about all art, written and visual, framing things in such a way that we pay attention to them. "The frame does not change the moment, but it changes our way of perceiving the moment. It makes us NOTICE the moment, (p. 15)" he says. Good writing is all about what we choose to frame.

## Long shot:

*We can see the whole person head to toe, or a setting in its entirety.*

This kind of shot can be achieved in writing by focusing on the "big picture." This can be used in fiction to establish setting, and in essays to establish the situation in a particular place.

## Medium shot:

*Subjects are filmed from the waist up. We see about half of the subject. This is the most common shot.*

When I draw my comic strip, nearly all the frames I draw are medium shots. Unless a character is running or jumping or doing something else that requires I show his or her whole body, most of the information I need to get across in a scene can be accomplished with a character's facial expressions and hand gestures.

## Close-up:

*The subject fills nearly the entire frame. This is often a character's face but can also be an object.*

Focusing on a person's face can draw attention to his or her emotions. Focusing on a person's hands can cause us to observe closely exactly what he or she is doing. Focusing on an object can emphasize its importance and tell us something about its owner, or the situation we are taking in as a whole.

## Extreme close-up:

*The camera focuses on a single small object or part of a subject (such as an eye or a lip), and it fills the entire frame.*

Everything I said about close-ups goes doubly here. If you are focusing on a person's eyes or eye, you need to have something very specific you are trying to convey. Even focusing on fingernails can tell us something. Is there dirt under them? What has the person been up to—burying a body? Have the nails been nibbled on? What is he or she nervous about?

9-1

| CINEMA TERMS | |
|---|---|
| **Camera Angles** | |
| Low | The camera is pointing up toward the subject, which can make the subject seem overpowering or menacing. |
| Straight on | The camera is at eye level with the subject being filmed. The most common angle. |
| High angle | Camera is high up, looking down on the subject of the frame. Can make the subject appear small or vulnerable. |
| **Lighting** | |
| Low key | Lighting is dim, emphasizing a contrast between light and shadows. |
| High key | Lighting is very bright and floods the picture. |
| Neutral key | Lighting is neutral, neither bright nor dark. |
| **Framing** | |
| Long shot | We can see the whole person head to toe, or a setting in its entirety. |
| Medium shot | Subjects are filmed from the waist up. The most common shot. |
| Close-up | The subject fills nearly the entire frame. This is often a character's face, but can also be an object. |
| Extreme close-up | The camera focuses on a single small object or part of a subject (like an eye or a lip), and the subject fills the entire frame. |

# Watching Movies/Movie Clips

One way to get students thinking about how to write cinematically is to have them watch film scenes, to analyze not only which types of shots are being used, but also why they are being used, as well as what effects the filmmakers were trying to create. I have read some debate about how films should be used in class. Some people view movies as a waste of time and an easy out for the teacher, which I suppose it is when you have *Kung Fu Panda* being shown in Algebra II class the day before spring break. Used correctly, though, films can be used not just to teach "critical viewing" but also to show students how writers and filmmakers make deliberate choices as they work.

Many teachers use short movie clips to teach specific film concepts. Other teachers have argued that just as you would seldom excerpt a single scene from a novel, you should watch movies in their entirety to see their full effect. I think both approaches can be valuable, if your viewing of the whole movie focuses on the literary aspects of the film, and if the movie clips are "close readings" of films with which the students may already be familiar. I emphasize to my students that movies are always *written* before they are filmed, and that just as everything in a book is there for a reason, every shot of a movie is written and then filmed the way it is for a reason. When we watch a clip in class, we analyze it on a chart like the one below:

9-2

| MOVIE-WATCHING CHART | | | | |
|---|---|---|---|---|
| Action/Image | Camera Angle | Framing/camera movement | Lighting/other effect | Effect created/ purpose of image |
|  |  |  |  |  |

We usually watch the clip one or two times straight through to get a feel for the scene, then slow down and watch it shot by shot, freeze-framing the DVD on each one to take down information. Here's how it might look for the "Imperial Fleet" scene near the beginning of *The Empire Strikes Back*.

| MOVIE CHART EXAMPLE | | | | |
|---|---|---|---|---|
| Action/Image | Camera angle | Framing/camera movement | Lighting/other effects | Effect created/ purpose of image |
| Star Destroyer in space, flying overhead | Low angle under ship's bridge | Close-up on space-ship | Medium key | Shows the size of the Star Destroyer— it is huge. |
| Star Destroyer flying toward camera, shadow passes over it | High angle | Long shot, ship moving toward camera | Low key— shadow mov-ing across Star Destroyer | Shows that some-thing even bigger is casting a shadow on the Star Destroyer |
| Shadow passing over the bridge of the Star Destroyer | Medium angle | Medium shot | Low key—shad-ow covers the entire bridge | Same as above |
| Star Destroyer under Vader's ship, which dwarfs it | Low angle | Long shot of Star Destroyer, but close-up of Vader's ship, which fills the entire frame | Low key | Shows that the gi-gantic Star Destroy-ers are dwarfed by Vader's even larger ship |
| Vader's ship flying through space, surrounded by little Star Destroyers | Medium angle | Long shot | Low key | Same as above |
| The back of Vader's helmet as he looks out at his fleet | Medium angle | Close-up | Low key | Makes Vader's entrance mysterious; we don't see his mask yet |
| Vader standing on the bridge, looking out the window | Medium angle | Long shot | Low key | Establishing shot; shows us what the bridge of Vader's ship looks like |
| Vader passes over his workers in the bridge pit; they look up fearfully | High angle | Medium shot— Vader in the fore-ground, workers in the background | Low key | The high angle makes Vader look intimidating; his min-ions look fearful and small from high up |

The point of exercises like this is to make students think about how every shot in a movie gives the audience information in a particular way, telling us things about setting, character, and plot, and creating emotional effects. Early scenes from a movie are especially useful, as they contain a lot of establishing shots and visual information for the audience to gather. Students may view a lot of movies, but they very seldom pay close attention to them. That alone is reason enough to do an exercise like this one occasionally. But the real purpose here is to get them writing. Once you've acquainted them with thinking like moviemakers, it's time to get students reading and writing like moviemakers.

# Finding Cinematic Writing

When we talk about cinematic writing techniques, I encourage my students to look for examples in books they are reading. Even books that predate or come from the early decades of cinema can be surprisingly movie-like. In C. S. Lewis's *The Silver Chair*, one of the Narnia Chronicles, there is a scene that is a perfect example of using camera angles. The main characters are caught in a blizzard, trying desperately to get to a castle where they have been told they will find shelter. As they cross a snow-blasted plain, they find their way into a series of trenches. We follow them down into the trenches, out of the wind, and see things from a low-angle perspective that creates a claustrophobic effect. They follow the trenches around several sharp angles, but always come to dead ends. Once they have succeeded in reaching the castle, one of the characters looks down from a high angle and sees that the trenches were actually gigantic letters from a message carved into the stones. Camera angle techniques can help present limited points of view and different perspectives.

# Picture Writing Exercises

What follows are a series of short, focused writing assignments to get students writing cinematically and thinking about what effects they can create by making a movie when they write.

## Camera Angles

This can be a tough camera technique to translate into writing, but it can come in handy sometimes in both fiction and nonfiction. Because "medium-angle" is a kind of default setting, a neutral, it doesn't work as well to focus on it in a writing exercise. Instead, I've done two exercises each for low- and high-angle shots.

**Low angle—People:** Write about a situation where you felt small and intimidated, either because you were young and adults towered over you, or because the situation itself was intimidating for whatever reason. See if you can describe a scene where you are forced to look up at people.

**High angle—People:** Write about a situation where you are "above" other people, either because you are taller, or because you are on stairs, on a balcony, or looking down from a window. What do you notice about other people when you are looking down at them? What perspective do you get? You can reverse the situation you wrote about from a low angle and write from the other person's perspective.

**Low angle—Setting:** Think of a specific place that was overpowering in its scale—a forest, a big building, a canyon, a huge roller coaster. Describe that place from a low angle and try to give your reader a sense of scale.

**High angle—Setting:** Write about being somewhere high, looking down and out over a place. It could be the top of the location you wrote about in the low-angle setting, but now you are looking down from the top of the tree, the building, the canyon. How does this change your perception of the place?

9-4

### Student Writing Samples: Camera Angles

**Low Angle People:**
I fell to the floor as a tall man rushed by, hitting me with a big box. It was Black Friday and I was shopping with my mom—that is, until we got near the toys. I got swept away by a crowd of people. I scrambled up and ran to find an opening. There were angry people with loaded carts coming at me from all sides. I yelled for my mom, but got no answer. All the people rushed around me as I ran. The crowed was never ending. I knocked into a bunch of Lego boxes and was free. I looked around frantically, searching.  ~ Helena Carey

**High Angle Setting:**
I stared out over the landscape. The houses that had once seemed quite large to me were now just a rainbow of pastel colors dotting the mountainsides. The cars that honked and swerved on the streets below were now smaller than toy cars. The large shopping plazas now matched the pictures of them on the town map. I could see eye to eye with every mountaintop. The tiny people down below, walking their miniature streets to their tiny houses, looked like ants. ~ Alexandra Finkle

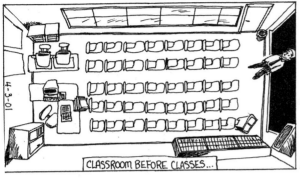

## Lighting

9-5

Lighting is a very tricky thing to create with words, and students are likely to get drawn into writing with adjectives. But if you think about memorable scenes from books, they are often lighted in particular ways, and that lighting is part of the atmosphere of the story. These four exercises try to use lighting to create opposite effects. Again, medium key has been omitted because of its neutral nature.

**Low-Key Creepy:** Write about a place with lots of light and shadow, a place that's at least a little bit creepy. It could be a forest, an old house, an alley. Focus on how the light hits, and doesn't hit, various objects in the setting. Nothing *has* to happen. You are just trying to create an atmosphere where something *might* happen.

---

### Student Writing Samples: Lighting

**Low-key creepy lighting:**
The school was coated in shadow. Shade fell over the now empty hallways. Moonbeams highlighted the courtyard, staining the world with ghastly shadows. Blackish-silver papers blew down the stairs; leaves rustled in the wind. The almost silence was eerie. The fence was almost hidden in shadow, partially lit in the light of the gibbous moon.
~ Calila Vignati

**Low-key magical lighting:**
The moonlight shone on the tall, snow-covered trees, casting shadows down on the white forest floor. An ice-covered lake sat in the distance. The snowy dock reached out into the center of the lake. The ice sparkled from the little amount of light shining onto the thin space that wasn't frozen. ~ Houston Crosley

**Low-Key Magical:** Write about a place with lots of light and shadow, a place that seems, well, magical. Think of a fairground, a nighttime forest with fireflies and starlight, a shimmering pool of water in the moonlight, a winter scene with snow falling, a sunrise or sunset. Describe the play of light and dark; make the scene seem inviting.

**High-Key Unpleasant:** Write about a place full of light that is not a place you want to be. Think of deserts, parking lots, over-lighted waiting rooms, or stores. Describe a place where the light itself is oppressive.

**High-Key Pleasant:** Write about a place full of light where you want to be: a field; a beach; an open, airy house; by a pool. Describe a brightly lit place and make your reader want to be there.

## Framing Exercises

9-6

Choosing what we place in our "frame" when we narrate something can focus readers' attention on what we want them to see—or conceal things we don't want them to notice. In an essay, choosing different frames can call our reader's attention to a problem or situation in a variety of ways. Here are two sets of exercises, one fiction, one nonfiction, that focus on framing.

### Framing Shots

This topic leaves a lot open to your students' imagina-

---

### Student Samples of Framing: Close-up on Hands

Her dirty hands brushed off the sand from the small object she had just discovered. It was a little toy carousel horse that had dirt here and there, but besides that, was beautiful. Its nostrils flared and it was forever running with nowhere to go and all day to go there. Her hands were trembling as she slowly petted it, even though she knew it was useless. The horse couldn't feel it. A drop of water landed on the horse's back, leaving a trail as it traveled down its stomach. Her hands were shaking so much that the horse looked like it was really galloping, running away from the sad memories. ~ Kelly Sutherin

Hiss! Hiss! The rough, pale hands grabbed another part of the sword, placed it on the anvil, and slammed it with the hammer, thus joining it to the hilt. Another pair of pale hands appeared, these ones younger-looking and smoother. This pair had a bellows and pumped the fire, increasing the temperature. The pair of rough hands appeared out of the shadows again and inserted the sword into the flames. Then an elfish voice said, "It is finished." ~ Travis Grover

tions, but also tightly focuses how they write and gets them thinking cinematically. The results usually range from amusing comedies to Hitchcockian thrillers.

- Write about someone hiding, finding, or making something, but focus your description only on the person's hands. Write only in "close-ups." Who the hands belong to, where they are, why they are doing what they are doing should remain a mystery. Imagine it as a movie scene where we are not supposed to know too much . . . yet.

- Write about the same events, but now write it as a series of "medium shots." This time you can show us the person from the waist up, focusing on the face, the kinds of expressions and gestures the character is making, the clothes he or she is wearing, and so on. We are given a lot more information.

- This time write the same events in "long-shot." You can show the whole character, head to toe, and also the setting. Where is the character? Describe the setting. What is he or she doing? Make it all clear now.

Combine "shots" this time. Rewrite the story one last time, but this time mix and match sentences to create a miniature movie scene. Do you start with close-ups and work out to long shots? Start with long shots and end with close-ups? Do you simply mix them up to reveal things as you see fit? Make us see your movie!

## Framing: Littering, Gum, or Cell Phones on Campus

As with the other techniques in this book, cinematic writing is not just for fiction. I know the topics listed above are a little bit "standardized testy," but bear with me. My object in choosing these particular topics is to get students thinking about "framing" a real-life problem visually. I give them the choice of these three topics, and tell them to write about the one they actually think is a problem on campus. The point is that they are trying to "show" the problem. These exercises might be a little shorter than the previous ones, maybe three or four sentences each. Combined, they might make a paragraph.

- Show your problem as a "long shot." Imagine you are standing across the street looking at your campus. What would you be seeing? What evidence of the problem would be evident?

- Show your problem as a "medium shot." If you were walking around campus, what would you be seeing as you walked right past people? What would you see as you sat in class?

- Show your problem as a "close-up." What could you show people's hands doing as they create the problem? What would it look like if you saw people's faces reacting to the problem?

- Show your problem as an "extreme close-up." If you had to focus on some very small items or actions that show your problem, what would they be?

One thing I always note with long shots is that they are often used as "establishing shots" in movies. Establishing shots are the opening shots of a movie or a particular scene that are the visual exposition of that scene—we see the setting from a distance and get an overall impression of it. Doing the same in writing can be useful in fiction to describe a setting, but establishing shots can also be used as grabbers in essays to "show" the big picture of a problem. (Note the Framing exercise on page 109 where you establish a problem by looking at a school campus from across the street.)

These exercises could even lead into longer essays or stories. Some of my students have taken the "hands in close-up" scenario in particular and run with it. But when the exercises are over, it's time to apply these techniques in real writing.

# Framing Pictures During the Writing Process: Making a Movie

When students are writing narratives, either real or made up, it is easier for them to create "word movies." But when they are writing essays, it is possible to use "movie writing" techniques as well. If we consider essays a kind of documentary or news story, it becomes easier to imagine images accompanying the main ideas being presented. The following are some suggestions for incorporating film techniques into the writing process.

## Prewriting

When students have chosen an essay topic or developed a plot for a story, they can start thinking cinematically before they start writing. I will sometimes ask students to take the chart they used for analyzing a movie clip and encourage them to use it as a template for brainstorming details in an essay or narrative. What scenes or ideas could be represented as longs shots, medium shots, or close-ups? How would the scene be lit? Are there any angles you would like to view a particular scene or subject from?

## Storyboarding

Another technique is to storyboard a narrative as if it were going to be a movie, or an essay as if it were going to be a documentary. Students can simply divide a paper into squares, then draw pictures representing the different "shots" they will be writing about, or you can supply them with ready-made storyboard frames (see Appendix, p. 140).

## Drafting

As students draft, they can again think of their story or essay as a movie or a documentary. I ask students to think every step of the way as they write, what "movie" do you want your reader to see? As they draft, I ask them to visualize the whole time, trying to create a movie as they write. I emphasize this especially when we're writing fiction, but if students are having trouble writing "visual" essays, I may especially encourage them as they draft to think of their essay as a movie.

## Revising

Once drafting is done and students are conferencing and revising, I may ask them to focus on this visual aspect of the writing as they share their writing with each other. Sometimes I will give them highlighters and ask them to mark either the sentences that create "movie shots" or the sentences that don't. I then ask them to discuss ways to make movies out of any sections of text that are hard to visualize. For instance, the essay opener, "Why should we have homework? We shouldn't!" doesn't create any images. If the opening is re-framed as a scene of a student who's supposed to be doing homework but is instead looking around the room at all the other things that are beckoning—video games, television, a skateboard, a good book, the pantry— we are given a picture of why this person thinks homework is a waste of time. It's important to note that "topic sentences," direct statements of your main ideas, aren't bad. They just need pictures added to them.

# Making Movies

The idea that they are making movies when they write is a powerful one for students. They tend to think of words as abstractions. When you fill up the page with a lot of words, you've done your job, right? But once students begin to think of themselves as filmmakers with words, it changes their perception of what writing is and what writing can do.

At the end of my young adult novel, *Making My Escape*, the protagonist, Daniel Finn, has been trying to make a science fiction movie epic—and his attempt has failed. His mentor gives him a notebook and a pen, and suggests that he can still make his movie—with words instead of film.

You don't need a cast and crew of thousands and Industrial Light and Magic to produce your special effects to create a movie. All you need are words and somewhere to record them.

# CHAPTER 10

# Pictures Beyond Compare: Figurative Language

**H**ere's a piece of figurative language to try on for size: "I was as nervous as a marshmallow in a campfire." Although it does have complexity on its side—it is both a simile and an example of personification, perhaps even anthropomorphism—it is not, in my book, a great example of figurative language.

It becomes even less impressive if you know its history. The *Orlando Sentinel* has recently run a series of articles by reporter Leslie Postal about the Florida Comprehensive Assessment Test in writing. It seems that certain standardized phrases and words are showing up in student essays from several areas of the state. One of those words is the exclamation "Poof!" Apparently the word *poof* is useful in nearly any writing situation, because it's appearing in many papers, thus earning them the name "Poof! Essays." One of the other frequently used standardized phrases in student "Poof! Essays" reads, "I was as nervous as a marshmallow in a campfire."

As Dave Barry says, I am not making this up.

I won't go into how wrong it is to teach standard phrases for use in standard essays, but I will venture to guess why this kind writing "instruction" is happening—especially as it pertains to our nervous marshmallow. For one thing, many people, including many teachers, view metaphors and similes as a cutesy, frilly window-dressing to "snazz-up" good writing. "Now, children, let's add some metaphors!"

Another reason formula metaphors are being taught is that good metaphors are hard to write. Because metaphors are hard to write, they can be seen as hard to teach. So, if something is hard to teach, and it's a frill, then your options seem to be: A. Don't bother teaching it, because student metaphors are invariably bad, or B. Teach them to write about nervous marshmallows.

I think there is another option—teaching students to use figurative language as real writers do.

# Figurative Language Is Essential

Figurative language is not an added topping on the ice cream sundae of our writing—like sprinkles or an extra cherry. Figurative language is inherent in the way we think about things, and we often resort to metaphorical language not as a way to add pizzazz to something, but because metaphors are the only way our minds can grasp certain abstract ideas. As Stephen Pinker points out in *The Stuff of Thought*, our founding document as Americans, the Declaration of Independence, talks of "the *bands* that *connected* the colonies to England, which it was necessary to *dissolve* in order to effect a *separation*" (235). The emphasis on the italicized words is Pinker's. Were there really bands that connected the colonies to England? Did those bands need to be "dissolved"? Most of us, myself included, have read the Declaration many times and been completely unaware of its metaphorical nature. That should tell us something—metaphors can be vivid, but they shouldn't necessarily stand out. They should flow naturally from the topic at hand. We tend to think of figurative language as something that must be carefully planned out, calculated, invented. In fact, we use figurative language all the time when we talk, without even thinking about it.

Consider these quotes from a National Public Radio story from October 1, 2008, titled "Senate Takes Up Bailout Bill." The story is about the economic downturn and government bailouts of business taking place at the time. It quotes a number of prominent political figures speaking about the situation:

**Senator Hillary Clinton:** This is a sink-or-swim moment for our country, and we cannot merely catch our breath. We must swim for the shores.

**Senator Judd Gregg:** We have a patient who has suffered a severe wound. They are bleeding profusely. We are going to try to put a tourniquet on that patient so that we can stabilize their condition.

**Senator Max Baucus:** A cloud hangs over the American economy. It's a cloud made up of a thousand failures, and it is casting a shadow over our country.

These are politicians, talking about something as down-to-earth and practical as the American economy, and they are all waxing metaphoric about it.

When I am doing lessons about figurative language, one of the things I do is ask my students to look for real-world examples of metaphors and similes in newspaper articles, in advertisements, in interviews, in comic strips. They are everywhere. And they are not a frill. Some things can only be understood in terms of metaphor.

As I stated in *Writing Extraordinary Essays*, "Carl Sagan in his book *Cosmos* compares the history of the universe to a calendar in which the Big Bang occurs in the first seconds of January 1st, and the entire history of the human race takes place during the last few seconds before midnight on December 31st. Here the metaphor is not only clearer than the numerical facts, but it also has the power to make us gasp" (Finkle, p. 61).

# Metaphors for All Occasions

The main distinction many people make when it comes to figurative language is between simile and metaphor. Similes use the word *like* or *as*. ("I was as nervous as a marshmallow in a campfire.") Metaphors are direct comparisons that don't use *like* or *as*. ("I was a marshmallow in a campfire.") I think of this as a rather shallow, technical distinction. I often use the term *metaphor* for both similes and metaphors, though my students, ever sharp, often point out to me that I am technically wrong. What interests me more, and what I try to teach my students, is the function of metaphorical language—the different ways it is used, and how those different ways influence the types of actual metaphors you use.

To say "use figurative language when you write" is like saying "use seasoning when you cook." Notice that simile I just used—it isn't a frill. It's essential for conveying my concept. Figurative language comes in many flavors, and using the wrong metaphor or simile in the wrong "dish" can leave a bad taste in your mouth.

So, let's take a look at the flavors we have to work with.

## Conceptual Metaphors

I have played around with different ways of getting students to think metaphorically. I've tried having them think small first—metaphors for the little things in their life, like their chores, or the messes in their bedrooms—and it usually falls flat. What usually works better, for me at any rate, is to start big. Really big. The first exercise in metaphorical thinking I use with students is actually drawn from Roger Von Oech's wonderful book about creative thinking, *A Whack on the Side of the Head.* The exercise is "Life is like . . . ." Students must come up with an object, activity, type of transportation, or other concrete noun that life is like. The simile must work not only as a metaphor, but as an extended metaphor; different aspects of the metaphor must lend themselves to comparison to different parts of life.

I put the topic on the board and ask students to think about possible metaphors. If students seem to be doing well on their own, I let them be, but if they are having trouble (which becomes apparent very quickly), I'll have us start to brainstorm possibilities on the board. I tell them they can use one of the possibilities we've generated, but the best life simile is one that comes from you and relates to your life. Do you play a sport? How is life like that sport? Do you dance, draw, run, play a musical instrument, or play video games? How is life like one of those activities?

How do the different parts of your activity relate to birth and death? Success and failure? Friends and enemies? What other aspects of life are included in your metaphor?

Students usually enjoy this exercise once they get into it, and some even expand it later into a full-fledged essay or even a poem (see Chapter 11). Some students will illustrate theirs, and most are eager to share them with the class. Some are odd, some are funny, but they all offer unique insights into both life and the writer's mind. A sampling of my students' metaphors is at right.

Life is like a staircase. Each day you make decisions that decide whether you move up or down. ~ Lucas Lyons

Life is like a block of tofu. It's bland unless you spice it up. ~ Jacob Tylec

Life is like a roller coaster. There's lots of twists, turns, ups and downs, some fun, some nauseating, but eventually the ride has to come to an end. ~ Alanna Scott

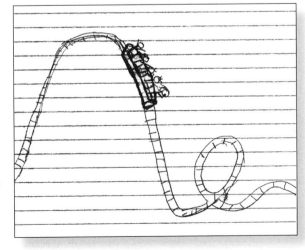

# Categories of Metaphors

Once we have completed this exercise, we try to apply conceptual metaphors to other big ideas, and we discuss how the simile controls our view of the subject at hand. Now that we've done some brainstorming, I sometimes give students an aid to metaphor-making—a chart to jump start their thinking. It is by no means complete—I'm always adding to it and amending it, and I encourage students to write all over it to add even more ideas. The Types of Metaphors chart, appears below (Figure 10-4). I designed this list to get students thinking about how many different ways there are to be metaphorical.

| TYPES OF METAPHORS | |
|---|---|
| **Categories of Metaphors** | **Examples** |
| Animals | Vertebrates, invertebrates, insects, worms, mollusks, fish, reptiles, birds, primates, rodents, marsupials, mammals, amphibians, marine mammals, house pets, platypuses |
| Art | sculpture, chisel, clay, drawing, painting, sketching, rough sketch, pens, paint brushes, paint, gallery, color, shading, perspective, light, contrast, composition, balance, abstract art, still life, portrait, landscape, paint-by-number |
| Business | small business vs. big business, bottom-line thinking vs. idealism, profit, debt, employees, employers |
| Cartoons | thought balloons, speech balloons, frames, joke, punchline, gag, security blanket |
| Computer | hard drive, software, Internet, e-mail, monitor, screen, games, social network, instant messaging, graphics, blogs, World Wide Web |
| Food | main course/side dishes, courses (appetizers, entrée, dessert), types of food, seasoning, diets and feasts, fast food vs. gourmet, microwave instant food vs. homemade, junk food vs. health food, processed food vs. all-natural food, recipe |
| Historical | Prehistoric, ancient Greek, Roman, medieval, Renaissance, Reformation, revolutions, wars, battles, rulers, dictators, kings, presidents, prime ministers, documents, constitutions, laws, movements |
| Home | living room, dining room, kitchen, bathroom, bedroom, study, family room, house, mansion, estate, apartment, door, window, roof, walls, floor |
| Literary | David and Goliath, Joan of Arc, Romeo and Juliet, The Good Samaritan, Little Red Riding Hood, Cinderella, Jack (of the beanstalk fame) |
| Location | ocean, lake, stream, river, desert, forest, swamp, tundra, mountain, valley, jungle, city, country, small town, rural, farm, camp, cliff, gorge, school, work, hotel, theme park, hiking trail, other planets |
| Machine/invention | ships, cars, planes, train, steam roller, printing press, indoor plumbing, refrigerator, oven, washer, dryer, blender, air conditioner, radio, television, computers, light bulbs, harnessed electricity, cameras, movies, video tape, digital photography |
| Mathematical | counting, adding up, subtracting, multiplying, dividing, graphing, distributing, unknown, negative, positive, problem, solution, finite, infinite |

| Medical/ health | blood loss, diagnosis, disease, germs, cancer, tumor, resuscitation, surgery, bandage, stitches, rescue, CPR, defibrillator, life support, ambulance, emergency room, exercise, eating right, medicine, prescription, cure-all |
|---|---|
| Music | concert, orchestra, marching band, rock band, instruments, percussion, piano, virtuoso, vocalist, off-key, pitch-perfect, song, symphony, score, sheet music |
| Nature | Trees, flowers, weeds, gardens, fields, lawns, grass, weather (see below), ecosystem, seeds, plants, predator, prey, natural balance, extinction |
| Retail | sale, bargain basement, designer, special, brand name, store brand, generic, box store, mom-and-pop store, dollar store, check-out, club store, grocery store |
| School | classes, period, class changes, students, teachers, principals, hall monitors, parents, desks, rows, groups, media center, main office, worksheets, assignments, packets, tests, quizzes, exams, standardized tests, grades, letter grades, averages, lesson plans, lessons, lectures, labs |
| Science | gravity, magnetism, atoms, time, relativity, entropy, inertia, proof, experiment, hypothesis, results, momentum, velocity, acceleration |
| Space | stars, planets, black holes, supernovae, asteroids, comets, dark matter, galaxies, universe, star clusters, orbits, gravitational pull, nebulae, Big Bang, red giants, white dwarfs |
| Sports | game, ball, goal, winning, losing, playing, rules, bases, defense, offense, good sportsmanship, poor sportsmanship, coaches, players, benchwarmers, star players, fans, trades, time-outs |
| Storytelling | plot, exposition, rising action, climax, falling action, resolution, conflict, protagonist, antagonist, setting, characters |
| Theater | stage, players, entrances, exits, cast, actor, major role, bit part, lines, direction, center stage, spotlight, sets, costumes, props, scripts, rehearsal, performance, audience, critics |
| Theme park/ amusement park ride | roller coaster, merry-go-round, tilt-o-whirl, water flume, kiddie ride, race cars, flying elephants, falling elevator ride |
| Weather | sunshine, rain, clouds, wind, snow, ice, hurricanes, tornadoes, monsoons, storms, lightning, thunder, overcast, floods, heat, cold |

After distributing copies of this chart, I give students a series of topics to help them brainstorm metaphors. What is school like? A factory or a laboratory? A buffet or a school cafeteria? What would school be like if you compared it to nature? or music? or food preparation? Here are some other "big idea" fill-in-the-blanks I use to get students thinking metaphorically and developing the metaphors:

- Reading is like . . .
- Writing is like . . .
- The Internet is like . . .
- TV is like . . .
- Polluting the world is like . . .

- Staying angry at someone is like . . .
- Friendships are like . . .
- Families are like . . .

Real-world items from one part of the chart above might be compared metaphorically to items on another part. Looking at storytelling and weather, what is the weather of a plot line? What is the plot structure of a storm? How is a business like an ecosystem? How is a marching band like a solar system?

Sometimes students choose to develop one of these exercises into a complete piece of writing. After doing exercises like these, metaphors and similes are no longer a frill. They are sometimes the main event.

## Descriptive Metaphors

Once we have the idea that figurative language can be about big ideas, not just a frill, we discuss the fact that metaphors are not used only to describe big concepts. They can indeed add life and vividness to specific descriptions. Students tend to think of figurative language as something we use in poetry, especially to describe "pretty things." Actually, metaphors have a variety of uses—some pretty, some decidedly not pretty.

Many of the exercises below I use simply as one-sentence writing exercises at the beginning of class to get students thinking of new metaphors.

## Sound Metaphors

We discussed sensory language in Chapter 3. We return to the topic briefly here, because when writers deal with the senses, the best tool they have at their disposal is metaphor. If you are making a movie or radio show, you can have your sound effects person create sounds. All writers have is words, but words can be figurative—they can evoke more than the literal.

If you want students to use sensory metaphors, have them read some Ray Bradbury; there is no one finer for writing metaphorical prose. In his frequently anthologized science fiction short story, "All Summer in a Day," Bradbury describes the planet Venus as a place where it rains all day. But he gives us a sense of what that endless sound must be like. He describes it as "the tatting drum, the endless shaking down of clear bead necklaces up on the roof, the walk, the gardens, the forests." Pick nearly any Ray Bradbury story and you'll have opportunities to discuss metaphors. Every page of his prose teems with them!

A fun resource for getting students to write figuratively about sound is the National Public Radio show "Vocal Impressions: Hearing Voices." The show plays recordings of famous people with unique voices, then asks readers to describe the voices using "poetic" language.

If you go to npr.org, you can search for "Vocal Impressions" and find examples both in print and as podcasts. If you play students one or two of the better-known voices, then share the metaphors that go with them, you can then play other recordings and have students come up with their own figurative language.

Some examples from the show:

Sean Connery's voice is described by listener Heather Carol as "The sensation of dipping your hand into a big, black bag of marbles."

Mae West's voice is described by Leslie Ott as "A pigeon from New Jersey that learned to talk."

In trying to get students to describe sounds figuratively, I ask them to describe various events and settings in terms of figurative sound. Some other exercises I use include the following:

- The noisy party sounded like . . .
- The storm sounded like . . .
- The wind in the trees sounded like . . .
- The raging river sounded like . . .
- The amusement park sounded like . . .

If you read that it rained really loudly, that doesn't help you hear the rain. If you say the rain rumbled across the lake like an approaching freight train—that helps us hear it.

## Atmospheric Metaphors

Metaphors help create any kind of atmosphere, not just beautiful ones. And even metaphors about beauty can have a whimsical quality about them. Years ago a college friend of mine coined the simile that a full moon mostly obscured by clouds looked "like an eraser smudge in the sky." It did indeed, and to this day, when we such a moon, someone in our family will remark on it in precisely those words. "Look! The moon is an eraser smudge in the sky!"

I emphasize to my students that different metaphors can create different kinds of atmosphere or mood. A bare tree in the fog can be neutral. A bare tree looming like a tall, misshapen giant creates an atmosphere—sinister. A bare tree with delicate black-lace branches creates a very different atmosphere.

To give students a chance to work with atmospheric metaphors, I give them a setting, and then an atmosphere they should try to create using figurative language. I give students a list of several different kinds of atmosphere:

| | | | | |
|---|---|---|---|---|
| Sinister | Magical | Gloomy | Humdrum/boring | Spooky |
| Festive | Majestic | Gothic | Lush | Oppressive |
| Pleasant | | | | |

Next I give them a setting and ask them to describe that place figuratively, so that it creates atmosphere.

You could take one object and create several kinds of atmosphere, or take one type of atmosphere and create it using several different metaphorical descriptions of settings.

Settings might include:

| | | | |
|---|---|---|---|
| A tree | An old building | A roller coaster | An old office building |
| A classroom | A street | A front porch | A skyscraper |
| A path in the woods | A hallway | A kitchen | A canyon |

For example, a spooky roller coaster might be a large, dark, uncoiled snake, waiting to claim its next victim. A majestic roller coaster might tower like a cathedral, gleaming in the sunlight.

## People Metaphors

Describing people metaphorically can give our readers additional insight into their personalities and appearances—sometimes flattering, sometimes not. I am careful to emphasize to students that descriptions of people, figurative or not, need to be fictitious if they're unflattering.

If we are describing how people or characters look, the choice of metaphor can give us an immediate impression that lasts. Dolores Umbridge from *Harry Potter and the Order of the Phoenix* is one of the most despicable characters in recent fiction, and our first impression of her is created by a metaphor. Harry thinks she "looked just like a large, pale toad . . . Her eyes were large, round, and slightly bulging. Even the little black velvet bow perched on top of her short curly hair put him in mind of a large fly she was about to catch on a long sticky tongue" (146).

Since describing people's looks can get a bit mean-spirited, I tend to encourage students to concentrate on describing attitudes metaphorically. I ask them to look at the master list of metaphor topics and write metaphors to describe a person who is one of the following: overly busy, lazy, very social, shy, distracted, focused, loud, klutzy, gentle, grouchy, or sleepy.

If you consider how these people might be compared to animals, to weather, or to things in space, there are quite a lot of possibilities.

## Figurative Grossness

Metaphors are not always pretty; in fact, in the right context, they can be downright disgusting. Middle schoolers like disgusting. So we actually talk about contexts in which your metaphors might be vivid, but not pretty. I include these because sometimes gross metaphors are a way to add humor to a piece, or to make a topic particularly vivid. In Wally Lamb's short story "Severance," he talks about a boy who is tripped and falls forward onto the pavement. The first-person narrator describes him as having a "raw meat chin." That description never fails to elicit a collective "Ew!" from students.

What makes a gross metaphor truly gross, ironically, is that it must be "fresh." The metaphor must be not only be gross—it must also be vivid, and give a different way of looking at the subject at hand. To say a room looked like a tornado went through it is a cliché. To say the room looked like a giant dog tried to eat all the room's contents and then threw them back up is—well, fresh. Ew.

Prompts for Gross Similes:

- The disgusting dinner was like . . .
- The ugly clothes looked like . . .
- The messy room looked like . . .
- The skinned knee looked like . . .
- The exploded garbage bag was like . . .
- Her stuffy nose was running like . . .

These kinds of metaphors are not for the faint of heart, and not necessarily for right before or after lunch, but students eat them up. Figuratively speaking, that is.

# Hyperbole

The last category of figurative language I try to cover with students, one that is often neglected as a writer's tool, is hyperbole. The amazing usefulness of hyperbole cannot be overstated. Okay, it can. But hyperbole often creates pictures and catchy, funny phrases that stick in a reader's head. Sometimes hyperbole is a good idea (humor essays) and sometimes it's a bad idea (résumés). But when it's a good idea, it can make a point and make readers laugh.

My favorite writer of humorous overstatements is Dave Barry. Consider the Barry-isms below. The first two come from Barry's essay about Disney World, "Attack of the Cartoon Animal Heads."

Barry says that he drove through south central Florida, a region that in recent years has "sprouted dozens of . . . communities with names like Belle Harbour Vista Manour Downes Estates Centre West II . . . ." We know this name is an exaggeration, but we also know exactly what he means. We've seen those developments. He later refers to Disney World as a place where the "restrooms are clean enough for neurosurgery."

In his essay about video games, "Un-Nintended Benefits" Barry writes that his character in any video game dies almost instantly, "whereas my son can keep the little man alive through several presidential administrations."

In his essay "Confessions of a Weenie" he says that, "When I was a child, I was routinely terrified by horror movies, even the comically inept ones where, when Lon Chaney turned into a werewolf, you could actually see the makeup person's hand darting into the picture to attach more fake fur to his face."

In the spirit of Dave Barry, here are some topics your students can go "over the top" about.

## Hyperbole of Size

The room was so small . . .    The classroom was so crowded . . .

The living room was so large. . .    The restaurant buffet was so long . . .

The campus was so large . . .    The car was so big . . .

The car was so small . . .

## Hyperbole of Senses

The lights were so bright . . .    The woods were so dark . . .

The party was so loud . . .    She was such a soft speaker . . .

The smell was so nasty . . .    The kitchen smelled so good . . .

## Hyperbole of Action

He was such a fast runner . . .    He walked so slowly . . .

She could jump so high . . .    He talked so fast . . .

He was so nervous . . .    He texted on his cell phone so fast . . .

He gobbled his food so quickly . . .

# A Main Ingredient

Figurative language is not just a seasoning—it can be a main ingredient that adds life and vividness and new insight to even the most humdrum topics.

# CHAPTER 11

# Pictures as Poetry: Evoking Emotion

I began *Writing Extraordinary Essays* with a cartoon about students and poetry.

My point was that students need to read a genre to write a genre, whatever that genre may be. I segued into essay writing in that book, but here I am going to stick with poetry for a bit. Many students never read poetry, yet love to write it. Because they never read poetry, they have some mistaken ideas about what poetry is and does. When I teach poetry, I begin by asking students to define it. They nearly always write something along these lines: "Poetry is writing about emotions," or "Poetry is a way to express your feelings." In other words, poetry is about the vague world of "feelings"—it is all about abstractions.

These feelings are often either overly flowery or hyperbolically depressing in student poems. In the cartoon strip I have two student poets who represent these two poetic extremes: Gail Goth and Candy Sweet, arch rivals of poetry.

When students actually read published poetry (something they often resist doing on their own), they find that although there are, indeed, a lot of emotions, most published poetry is about *specifics*—more specifically, poems tend to be word pictures that make abstract ideas concrete. Look at Robert Frost. Two of his most famous poems, "Stopping by Woods on a Snowy Evening" and "The Road Not Taken," are about nothing less than our journey through life. Yet those two poems are about two different, specific ways of looking at our journeys through life.

I tell students that poems often avoid stating feelings directly; instead, they *evoke* feelings. One of the definitions of *evoke* on my laptop dictionary says it means "to bring to mind a memory or feeling." But there is another meaning I like even better. To evoke is to "make beings appear who are normally invisible," as is in evoking a spirit.

The idea of making invisible things visible is enormously helpful. Feelings and ideas are invisible until they are attached to concrete things. Poetry, more than any other kind of writing, is about this relationship between the abstract and the concrete—and students are often incredibly oblivious to this fact.

What follows in this chapter are some suggestions for getting students to write poetry that is specific . . . and evocative. I need to admit up front that I am not a huge fan of the typical "Poetry Notebook" with lots of easy formula poems that get assigned, written, and graded quickly. The poems, such as acrostics, are fun to write and easy to grade, but often tend to be a bit shallow. I'm not against having fun when writing by any means, but sometimes the fun comes from writing something challenging. Real poetry is a challenge—probably the most painstaking kind of writing there is—yet we often make students think of it as a blow-off assignment they can dash off in five minutes.

The poem ideas I'm going to delve into here are sometimes quick, but sometimes involve an investment of time. Although poetry writing is not valued on any writing tests I know of, it is a kind of writing many students find themselves drawn to. I think they deserve to learn some of the craft.

# Read Poetry to Write Poetry

It is beyond the scope of this chapter to examine the age-old conundrum of how you teach poetry (or any literature for that matter) so you neither skimp on the "technical stuff" nor dissect the writing to the point that it's dead on the table and no longer brings any pleasure. If I had to chose, I'd say read for pure enjoyment, but I still think you are missing out on a large part of a poem if you can't appreciate some of the effort that went into creating it. I'd like to suggest a middle ground between ignorant enjoyment and scholarly dissection. That middle path is reading like a writer.

Before I delve into poetry with students, I try to at least teach them about picture basics (nouns and verbs) and about figurative language in general. When we read poetry in my class, I emphasize at every turn that poetry is about the specific—about the pictures. If we have consumable copies of the poems in a workbook or from the public domain, we highlight everything that's specific. We discuss how the details are both literal and figurative. The road not taken is a road, but it is also a path through life. When the poem says there are "miles to go before I sleep," sleep is sleep, but sleep is also death. This sounds like simple stuff, but I think students really need to hear it repeated over and over so they get the message that poems are pictures. Sometimes the picture points to something more, and sometimes, as Frederick Buechner points out, the poem exists simply to put a frame around a moment (p. 15).

We also take a look at how rhythm and meter work, how a rhyme scheme works, and what a rhyme is (it's not, despite what many pop songs promote, putting "together" and "forever" at the end of adjacent lines). I emphasize that we are going over these concepts both to appreciate the effort that goes into creating poetry and also to provide students with tools they can use in their own poetry. But it always comes back to the pictures. How can you take a simple image or event and make it poetry?

Most literature books have a fairly decent collection of poetry, but there is plenty of public domain poetry to be found online, and there are some excellent collections available online and in bookshops as well. One of my favorites is Garrison Keillor's collection titled simply *Good Poems*. I am not going to list many examples here—there are too many to do justice to the variety. What I do recommend is finding poems that fit the types of poetry students will be writing—read narrative poems before writing narrative poems, for example.

# Creating Picture Poems

• • • • • • • • • • • • • • • • • • • • • • • • • • • • • • • • • • • • • • • • • • • •

The following are types of poems I have had my students write—usually with very visual and vivid results.

## "I Am From" Poem

This assignment is a formula poem—I admit it. But I think it is a powerful one for getting students to think in terms of specifics. Although I found it in Mary Pipher's book *Writing to Change the World,* it was inspired by George Ella Lyon's poem "Where I'm From," which you can read at http://www.georgeellalyon.com/where.html.

The "I Am From" poem follows a very simple formula. Each line begins with the words "I am from," and ends with a specific detail from the person's life. "I Am From" poems do not need to rhyme or follow any kind of meter—but they do need to be specific. Each line is a specific "thing" from your life that either made you who you are or explains who you are. My poem reads like this:

**"I am from"**

D. Finkle

I am from Round Lake, where there is a round lake and narrow streets and tiny Victorian
    cottages.

I am from the house on top of the hill

The hill I had to walk up after every school day,

And struggle up after every bike ride.

I am from Dutch Finkles

And Irish FitzGeralds.

I am from hot New York summers with wide open windows

And box fans roaring in the corner of the room.

I am from crisp New York autumns ablaze in colored leaves.

I am from bitter New York winters and the hope of snow days.

I am from muddy New York springs that melted but stayed cold.

I am from Star Trek and Star Wars.

I am from Lego spaceships three feet long and stories I made up about them that were

three months long.

I am from bookshelves and books, especially books with maps.

I am from Narnia and Middle Earth.

I am from the comics section of the paper.

I am from my own private cartoonist's studio in the corner of my room.

I am from drawing pens and bottles of India ink.

I am from empty cartoon frames filled with possibilities.

This poem is a great way to start the year, especially if you want to get to know your students. Simply write one of your own, or use mine, to demonstrate how it's done, and set them to work. You will be amazed by the power of the results, and every line will be a picture.

## "Found in My Portfolio" Poem

Most instructions for Found Poems ask students to find a piece of text someone else wrote—a newspaper column, an advertisement, a comic strip speech bubble, and so on—and turn it into a poem by breaking up the lines. In my class, if they've been at the school any length of time, I ask them to pillage their writing folders and find a piece of prose from their essays to make into a "Found Poem."

I try to convey two things with "Found in My Portfolio" poems. One, that poems are about specific subjects, just as prose pieces need to be. I point out that the piece they choose should be a paragraph about something specific—an event or a description of something; otherwise it won't make a good poem. Two, I point out the only hard and fast rule about what a poem is: a piece of text in which the words are broken up into something other than traditional paragraphs. The minute you break a paragraph into shorter lines to create "special effects," it's a poem.

When I model creating a Found Poem, I take something I've written—even an innocuous e-mail—and project it on my classroom screen. I then hit "enter" to break up the lines of the paragraph into different poetry lines. I point out that longer lines with more words create speed, and a buildup of suspense. Shorter lines or one-word lines make the reader stop. They create emphasis. A word all alone on a line stands out.

Whenever I do this assignment, I am floored at the quality of the work. Just by breaking up the lines differently, students turn a paragraph into a poem that really works . . . a poem that is visual.

> **"I Am From" Student Samples**
>
> I am from Pam and Jim Sanders, who have been in love for 25 years.
> I am from a metropolis called Orlando and a solid wood house with less than five rooms
>   cluttered with harsh months come and gone.
> I am from the belief that you can live off fruit smoothies and Ramen Noodles chicken-flavored soup. ~ Karen Sanders
>
> I am from a four-bedroom house in the middle of nowhere. I am from the Pennsylvania Falls where the leaves change colors.
> I am from the Titanic.
> I am from a swimming pool in Grandma's backyard.
> I am from the magic Q-Ball . . . I always have the answer.
> I am from my DJ's studio in the garage.
> I am from Barbie's Cooking Kitchen and from "Dragon Tales." ~ Alisia Lynch

## Narrative poem

A narrative poem is simply a poem that tells a story. I encourage students to take an incident from their lives or make up a short piece of fiction, and then turn it into a poem simply by breaking up the lines. Having read narrative poems such as Alfred Noyes's "The Highwayman" and Robert W. Service's "The Cremation of Sam McGee," however, many students want to take their poems a step further and make them rhyme.

What I'll say about rhyming here can apply to any of the poems I discuss below. First, I tell students not to build a poem around the rhymes. It might work if you're shooting for silly (which is okay sometimes!), but for most poems, simply writing to the next rhyme that comes along leads to "I love you/The sky is blue/I lost my shoe," nonsense.

I encourage my students to draft a rough version of their poem as a paragraph, and then make a Found Poem out of it. Once they've broken it into lines, I ask them to brainstorm potential rhyming words—words that rhyme and might make sense in the context of the narrative. One way to brainstorm rhymes is to run through the alphabet in your head, I tell them, looking for a rhyming word or two at each letter. If a student is looking for a rhyme for "new," she begins at "a" (no rhyme there) then goes to "b" (*blue* rhymes), and on to "c" (*cue, clue*). I also keep a few rhyming dictionaries around my room—the Merriam-Webster pocket-size is the best. It's user-friendly with the rhymes for any given sound all in one place. Be warned—it is hard to keep rhyming dictionaries in your classroom.

Once students have brainstormed rhymes, they can then begin to structure their poem, putting rhyming words at the end of lines. This practice of ending lines with rhymes sounds like an obvious thing, but it's something to note as standard practice as you read poems. An astonishing number of students write poetry as prose, with the rhyming words all over the page in the middle of lines.

I cannot promise that these poems will all be masterpieces, or that the rhymes will all be graceful. I *can* guarantee that trying to create a rhyming poem that tells a story will stretch students' skills as writers and give them a new appreciation for the work that goes into writing poetry. It will also help them write poetry that is specific and concrete rather than abstract.

## Place Poem

Using the same methods above, students can write a poem about a favorite place, or a place that has meaning to them somehow—whether positive or negative. They can write their description in prose, then break it up into poetry. They can make it rhyme or not rhyme, depending on what you require, or on their taste.

## Object Poem

Nearly everybody has an object that means something to them. In this assignment I ask students to pick an object that they have "history" with—that has been with them through good times and bad—and write about it. I tell them about a drawing table my Uncle Mike made for me when I was in high school. I used to draw cartoons on it every night, but then I left it behind when I went to college and only used it when I was home for the summer. Eventually I left it behind for years when I moved to Florida, but when I remodeled a shed behind our house to be my studio, my mother brought the table south, and now it's mine again.

I've had students write poems about musical instruments, sports equipment, clothes, toys, and other objects, some of them odd. What they all have in common is that they are moving without ever mentioning an emotion—and they are all specific.

## Emotion Poem

Speaking of emotions, I eventually return to them because so many students think that emotions are what poetry is all about. They are right. The challenge I give them here is to write a poem about an emotion without ever using the "emotion word." Write about sadness, but don't use the word *sad*.

We begin by listing emotions on the board—there are a lot of them, including variations such as *annoyed, angry, mad,* and *livid*. In many ways, this is a variation on the emotion activities from Chapter 6. I ask students to chose an emotion and think of a time they've felt it, or to write about a fictitious situation. They then need to show the emotion without ever telling us what it is. Again, the writing may be rhymed or unrhymed, and I often ask students to start with prose and transform it. The results usually transcend somewhat "gushy" poems many students are prone to.

# Concrete Abstractions

At its worst, student poetry can be overwrought, yet vague. But at its best, student poetry can make abstract ideas tangible. This, of course is what all good writing does—it makes abstractions concrete.

• • • • • • • • • • • • • • • • • • • • • • • • • • • • • •

# CHAPTER 12

# The Big Picture: Why Details Matter

I began this book by talking about my relationship with comic strips, which were my first experience with words and pictures. I return to that relationship now. Legendary *Peanuts* creator Charles Schulz has said that casting a comic strip is like creating a piano keyboard. It "should have a variety of personalities so that you are not always striking the same note. You must have a full keyboard on which to play out the themes and variations demanded each day" (1975, p. 91).

I can relate to this as a cartoonist, but the image of a full keyboard upon which to play out themes and variations also struck me as appropriate as I reach the end of this book. When my students write, I want them to have a "full keyboard" of types of images. I want them to be able to choose the right kinds of pictures for the right topics. Depending on what they are writing about, students may need to describe events, people, places, or situations. To describe those things, they may need to engage the senses, create movies, or use metaphors.

As we move beyond exercises and discuss either assigned writing or writing workshop pieces with topics of students' own choosing, we talk frequently about planning ahead, figuring out what kinds of word pictures and details will suit their topics. One tool I will sometimes give them is a prewrite paper on which they can brainstorm which kinds of details, and what specific details, they might be able to use when they begin drafting.

As my students move beyond exercises, I tell them I want them to be able to take any abstract

### Essay Prewrite Worksheet

| WORD PICTURES | |
|---|---|
| **Nouns** | **Verbs** |
| | |

**Movie details:** Your topic as…
**Long shot**

**Well-placed list:**
What ideas could appear as a list of specific details?

**Medium shot**

**Descriptions of people:**
(Looks, actions, personalities, emotions)

**Close-up**

**Extreme Close-up**

**Figurative Language**
My main idea is like:

**Hypothetical situations:**
If I had my way:

My supporting ideas are like:

If my opposition has their way. . .

**Hyberbole**
Exaggerated details. . .

concept and make it concrete. And so my most advanced exercise for students short of their real essay writing is to give them a series of abstractions and see what they can do with them to make them concrete. I want students to take abstractions and "play" them with the full keyboard of word pictures.

I'll put a single word on the board and tell students to make it concrete. If I feel that it's a particularly challenging word, I'll give them some questions to guide their thinking. Here's a list of some of the words I use. I'm sure you could find more of your own.

I ask students to take these ideas and not just define them, but to create pictures of them. I tell them to show these words at work in people and in places, with metaphors and with movies. Each person who writes about Envy or Success or Play will have a different set of pictures to give us. This is my ultimate goal—to have them be able to take any topic and make it concrete, the way a stand-up comedian can take any page of the phone book and somehow, reading from it, make it funny. I want them to play the full keyboard. But until they've seen that keyboard played in real writing, and practiced using those tools for themselves, they are unlikely to use them when it really matters.

When does it really matter? When they write for real.

12-2: This list of abstract concepts can be used as writing prompts. Challenge students to take one of the abstractions and make it concrete.

### ABSTRACTIONS

| | | |
|---|---|---|
| annoying | freedom | lies |
| art | friendship | music |
| busy | fun | names |
| comedy | games | nature |
| compassion | happiness | play |
| cruelty | hate | power |
| creativity | home | success |
| dreams | imagination | time |
| enemy | joy | truth |
| envy | judgmental | work |
| evil | laughter | |

# Real Writing

The exercises in this book are just that—exercises. They aren't meant to be full-fledged writing assignments, though some of them might develop into full-length pieces.

Real writing is where the pictures really count. If the exercises I've presented here are sketches, then real writing is the full-color painting. The pictures really matter when students have something to say that really matters to them.

Note that the state writing test is not real writing. We are often pressured to believe it is, but as I tell my students, it is a really just a game we play. The pictures matter there, too, and are really the key to getting a high score. But the writing itself doesn't matter very much. As I said in a recent column I wrote for the *Orlando Sentinel*, standardized-test writing "has all the movement and appearance of writing without any of the things that make real writing real: real purpose, real topic, real audience, real effect on the real world . . . . I want my students to be involved, and aware, to care about things bigger than themselves. Writing can, in fact, help students discover and define what issues they care about" (Finkle, 2009).

How do we help students find those topics when they've been beaten down so far with prompts about gum chewing and school uniforms that they feel they have nothing to say? How do we find the real topics students care enough about to put their word pictures to use? My chief method for getting students to write for real is simple: I ask them to list things they love and things they hate. In *Writing Extraordinary Essays* I include some suggestions for helping students find topics they're passionate about, but that's a subject that, perhaps, deserves its own book.

## Words and Pictures: The Big Picture

Before I end, I will repeat one suggestion from *Writing Extraordinary Essays*. It is an assignment with the built-in potential for online publishing and a real audience. Every year I ask my eighth graders to write a "This I Believe" essay. "This I Believe" is no longer aired as a radio show on National Public Radio (unfortunately!), but continues as a Web site. The assignment is to create an essay of personal philosophy. The basic premise is that the personal philosophy must be expressed through word pictures and personal stories.

As students read and listen to some of the essays, we analyze them for their big ideas, the writers' beliefs, and the specific images that illustrate those beliefs. After they read ten or so of the essays in class (and sometimes more at home, since many students go on the Web site on their own time), I ask them to brainstorm their own beliefs and think about which ones might be illustrated by word pictures. For many students, this is the first time anyone has ever asked them to clarify what they believe about life.

Some students may be like Mr. Fitz in the cartoon below, however, and have so many beliefs they have difficulty choosing. But by encouraging them to chose the belief that is strongest and most personal, all students can eventually settle on one belief.

Once they settle on their beliefs and tie them to the circumstances of their lives, to the specific events that readers can picture, the results are usually nothing short of miraculous.

I end with the This I Believe assignment for two reasons. One, it's a great thought-provoking assignment that inspires everything we want to have happen for our students; it links real thought and insight to the specific pictures. Two, I wrote my own This I Believe essay around the time the radio show ended, and although it never made it on the air, I think it makes the perfect coda for this book. In the end, the relationship between big ideas and little pictures is about more than just writing.

# This I Believe

By David Lee Finkle

*I have always been fascinated by the relationship between words and pictures. I learned to read as a kid mainly so I could read the funnies on my own—especially Peanuts. Something about the combination of those abstract letters floating over those pictures appealed to me. I began to draw comic strips on my own, but it would take me years to discover why that original combination of words and pictures held such a deep appeal to me.*

*I'm now a middle school English teacher, and I try to teach my students that it's not enough to tell us when you write—you have to show us. It's all about the pictures. For instance, if I ask a class to write about a best friend, I will get a slew of generic essays: my friend is funny, fun, and nice. They all sound alike. But when I ask the class to create pictures, these friends suddenly come to life. Pictures appear. My friend and I try on crazy socks at J. C. Penney. My friend made me laugh so hard chocolate thick shake flew out my nose. My friend let me stay on his couch when my parents were fighting.*

*This is the oldest writing lesson in the world, but I've begun to realize that it is more than that. I assigned my eighth graders the task of writing "This I Believe" essays the past two years, and what I came to realize, reading their stories, seeing their beliefs, is that this idea of general and specific isn't just about writing. It's about life.*

*If I think about the kind of person I want to be, the main ideas I want to express with my life, the only way to live out those main ideas is to do specific things—to create pictures with my life. I can't just say I want to be a good father. I need to make a Rubik's Cube Halloween costume for my son or play a game with my daughter. I can't just say I want to be a good husband; I need to help with the dishes. I can't just say I want to be a good teacher; I need to take time to talk with students about their writing individually.*

*I ask my students, and myself, to think about what their pictures say about their lives. What do your specific pictures say about the main idea of your life? Do you even have a main idea?*

*I have come full circle; now I draw a comic strip about teaching for my local newspaper. Every day I take my general thoughts about education and turn them into words and pictures about pencils, gum, books, and students: abstract words floating over specific pictures. I believe that all of life is found in the balance between the general and the specific, the big idea and the little detail, the ideals we aim for and the actions that help us live out our ideals. It's all about the pictures we create with our lives, and what those pictures say.*

*This I believe.*

The pictures we create with our words and our lives, the stories we tell, have a power that bland generalities do not. At the end of one my favorite plays, Lerner and Loewe's *Camelot*, King Arthur is despondent that Camelot and the dream of the Round Table have come to an end. He says, "All we've been through for nothing but an idea! Something you cannot taste or touch, smell or feel; without substance, life, reality or memory" (111).

But then a boy named Tom shows up to inform Arthur that he wants to be a Knight, not because he has ever seen a knight, but because of "the stories people tell." He has been given a picture of what a knight is, what chivalry is, and because of it, wants to become a knight himself.

In the end, good writing enables us to pass along ideas worth sharing, by giving them substance, life, reality, and memory—by making them visual and vivid. It's all about the pictures.

# Plot Storyboard Template

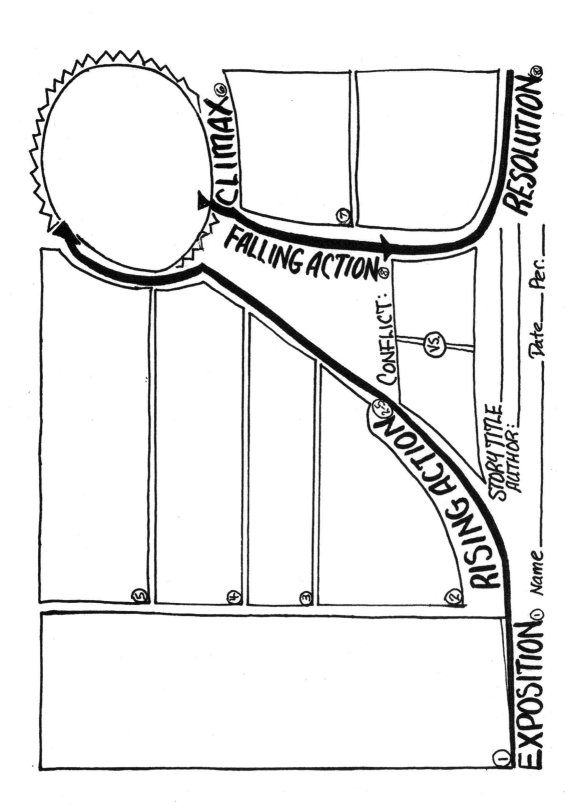

CLIMAX ⑥

RESOLUTION ⑨

FALLING ACTION ⑧

CONFLICT: ___ VS. ___

RISING ACTION

⑤ ④ ③ ②

EXPOSITION ①

STORY TITLE ___
AUTHOR: ___

Name ___
Date ___ Per. ___

# Suspect Templates

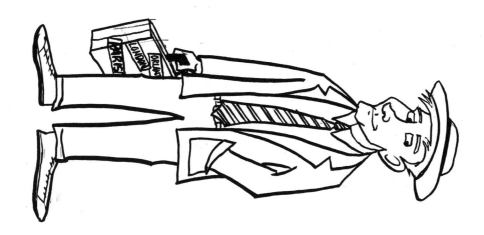

# Essay Prewrite Worksheet

| WORD PICTURES | |
|---|---|
| **Nouns** | **Verbs** |
| | |

**Movie details:** Your topic as...
**Long shot**

**Medium shot**

**Close-up**

**Extreme Close-up**

**Figurative Language**
My main idea is like:

My supporting ideas are like:

**Hyberbole**
Exaggerated details. . .

**Well-placed list:**
What ideas could appear as a list of specific details?

**Descriptions of people:**
(Looks, actions, personalities, emotions)

**Hypothetical situations:**
If I had my way:

If my opposition has their way. . .

# REFERENCES

Alexander, L. (1970). *The marvelous misadventures of Sebastian.* New York: E. P. Dutton and Company.

Avi. (1990). *The true confessions of Charlotte Doyle.* New York: Orchard Books.

Barry, D. (1994). *The world according to Dave Barry.* Avenel, NJ: Wing Books.

Block, M. (Writer). (2008, October 1). Senate takes up bailout bill. In NPR *All Things Considered.* Retrieved from http://www.npr.org/templates/story/story.php?storyId=95263484.

Bradbury, R. (1953). *Fahrenheit 451.* New York: Ballantine Books.

Buechner, F. (1988). *Whistling in the dark.* San Francisco: Harper San Francisco.

Clayton, J. B. (1992). The white circle. In W. Seabright (Ed.). *Junior great books series 7: Student anthology.* Chicago: The Great Books Foundation.

Essley, R., with Rief, L., & Rocci, A. (2008). *Visual tools for differentiating reading and writing instruction.* New York: Scholastic.

Finkle, D. L. (2002). *Making my escape.* Los Altos Hills, CA: May Davenport.

Finkle, D. L. (2008). *Writing extraordinary essays—Every middle schooler can! Strategies, lessons, and rubrics—plus proven tips for succeeding on tests.* New York: Scholastic Professional.

Finkle, D. L. (2009, September 17). Learning to write, sans FCAT. *Orlando Sentinel,* p. A15.

Finkle, D. L., & Finkle, C. D. (2009). *Portents.* DeLand, FL: Hairy Scary Ham Books.

Fulghum, R. (1988). *It was on fire when I lay down on it.* New York: Random House.

Hiaasen, C. (2009). *Scat.* New York: Knopf.

Jackson, S. (1991). The sneaker crisis. In *Prentice Hall literature bronze.* Upper Saddle Neck, NJ: Pearson Prentice Hall.

Keillor, G. (2003). *Good poems.* New York: Penguin.

Kurtz, G. (Producer), & Kershner, I. (Director). (1980). *Star wars episode V: The empire strikes back* [Motion Picture]. United States: Twentieth Century Fox.

Lamb, W. (1998). *I know this much is true.* New York: HarperCollins.

LeGuin, U. K. (1975). The rule of names. In *The wind's twelve quarters* (pp. 65–74). New York: Harper and Row.

L'Engle, M. (1980). *A ring of endless light.* New York: Farrar, Straus.

L'Engle, M. (1962). *A wrinkle in time.* New York: Farrar, Straus.

Lerner, A. J. (1961). *Camelot.* New York: Random House.

Lewis, C. (2004). *The chronicles of Narnia.* New York: HarperCollins.

Lowry, L. (1989). *Number the stars.* New York: Houghton Mifflin.

Lowry, L. (1993). *The giver.* New York: Bantam Books.

McCloud, S. (2006). *Making comics.* New York: HarperCollins.

McConnachie, B. (Commentator). (2007, April 30). Vocal impressions: Hearing voices, round four. In NPR *All Things Considered.* Retrieved from http://www.npr.org/templates/story/story.php?storyId=9914887

Oech, R. V. (1990). *A whack on the side of the head.* New York: Warner Books.

Orwell, G. (1983). *1984.* New York: Plume.

Pinker, S. (2007). *The stuff of thought.* New York: Penguin Books.

Pipher, M. (2006). *Writing to change the world.* New York: Penguin.

Postal, L. (2009, July 18). Poof! 'Template writing' on FCAT shows up in 12 school districts. *Orlando Sentinel.* Retrieved from http://articles.orlandosentinel.com/2009-07-18/news/fcat_1_poof-fcat-writing-essays.

Rowling, J. K. (2001). *Harry Potter and the prisoner of Azkaban.* New York: Scholastic.

Rowling, J. K. (2003). *Harry Potter and the order of the phoenix.* New York: Arthur A. Levine.

Schulz, C. M. (1975). *Peanuts jubilee: My life and art with Charlie Brown and others.* New York: Random House.

Schulz, C. M. (2006). *Happiness is a warm puppy.* Kennebunkport, ME: Cider Mill Press

Spiegel, A. (Writer). (2008, February 21). Old-fashioned play builds serious skills. In NPR Morning Edition. Retrieved from http://www.npr.org/templates/story/story.php?storyId=19212514.

Thurber, J. (1999). The night the bed fell. In *My life and hard times* (pp. 3–10). New York: Harper Perennial.

Ullman, J. R. (1988). *Banner in the sky.* New York: HarperTeen.

Watterston, B. (2005). *The complete Calvin and Hobbes.* Kansas City: Andrews McMeel Publishing.